BASIC BIBLE SERIES

OLD TESTAMENT
ROYALTY

HISTORY
OF   A
NATION

DAVID C. COOK PUBLISHING CO.

ELGIN, IL 60120

This Basic Bible Series study was developed through the combined efforts and resources of a number of David C. Cook's dedicated lesson writers. It was compiled and edited by Kelsey Menehan, designed by Melanie Lawson and Dawn Lauck, with cover art by Richard Sparks.
  —Gary Wilde, Series Editor

Old Testament Royalty: History of a Nation

© 1986 David C. Cook Publishing Co., 850 North Grove Ave., Elgin, IL 60120. Printed in U.S.A.

Scripture quotations, unless otherwise noted, are taken from the Holy Bible: New International Version, © 1973, 1978, 1984 by the International Bible Society, used by permission of Zondervan Bible Publishers.

ISBN: 0-89191-481-1
Library of Congress Catalog Number: 86-70888

Give us a king to lead us.

Contents

Like a Leaf in The Wind

Some of the most popular tourist attractions in the world are the ruins of ancient civilizations: the pyramids and sphinx at Giza, the Parthenon at Athens, the Circus Maximus at Rome. These engineering marvels are silent witnesses to the aspirations and dreams of peoples long dead. Their legacy continues in other areas, too: the Romans left us the idea of the republic and the rule of law; the Greeks left us the elements of science and philosophy.

However, the most influential and enduring monument we have is not an ancient ruin or the seeds of statecraft and logical thought. It is a Book—the Bible— the Jewish people's legacy to the ages.

While it contains each, it is not primarily a Book of philosophy or law or history: it is a Book of revelation. And that, as G. K. Chesterton says, "is not a philosophy because, being a vision, it is not a pattern but a picture. It is not a process, but a story. . . . In other words, it is exactly, as the phrase goes, like life."

This study looks at the Bible's account of the rise and fall of the nation of Israel through the lives of its kings. From a shepherd's tent to Solomon's "house of the forest of Lebanon" where the dishes were all pure gold, and, finally, to the fire-blackened ruins of the city of David, we follow the fortunes of a kingdom. Over it all there lingered the pronouncement of the aged prophet Isaiah: "we all do fade as a leaf; and our iniquities, like the wind, have taken us away."

Because it is revelation, the story is meant for us. Let it be ours to learn from, lest it be ours to follow.

1

A Power Struggle

Truth to Apply: As I trust God with my life, I begin to discover the difference between earthly power and God-given power.

Key Verse: Be sure to fear the Lord and serve him faithfully with all your heart; consider what great things he has done for you (I Sam. 12:24).

Why is it so hard for us to trust God to rule in every area of our lives? Is it because we are afraid we won't like the path He has chosen for us? Or is it because we want to see a more complete set of blueprints? (Not many of us like to move forward if we can't see the end of the trail.) Or could it be that, like the Israelites, we see our neighbors being successful in ways that we are not, and feel that their way of doing things is better than God's way?

Our culture admires an independent attitude, but it can lead us to close our ears to God's Word when we are told, "Trust in the Lord with all your heart and lean not on your own understanding; in all your ways acknowledge him, and he will make your paths straight" (Prov. 3:5, 6).

Trusting ourselves, a member of our family, or a friend, is often easier than trusting God. Why is this? How do you, personally, deal with this tendency?

Background/Overview: *I Samuel 12:14-25*

Politically, the events recorded in this passage represent a turning point for God's people. Israel changed from a tribal confederacy, with loose ties among the tribes, to a centralized government under a king.

For almost 400 years the tribes had been ruled by judges and elders. God was the one uniting force among the tribes, and since the time of Moses, the Israelites had viewed Him as their King.

But the tribes were never very willing to cooperate, except when helping each other fight common enemies. They quarreled among themselves, disobeyed the judges God put over them, and copied the ways of neighboring peoples. As they conquered Canaanite tribes, the Israelites adopted strange gods.

The Philistines were the major source of concern to God's people. These invaders from the sea had firmly settled in the fertile plain between the hills of Judah and the Mediterranean shore. Their five city-states were ruled by kings, each of whom supported the others in military and political matters.

Because the Israelites were defeated again and again by the Philistines, they decided a king of their own was the answer to their problems. A king could lead them to battle and bring them victory. So it was that Samuel, the last of the judges chosen by God, bridged the transition to Israel's first monarch.

Light on the Text

The Choice (12:14, 15)

Samuel was an old man when he placed a choice before the people of Israel: obey the Lord God and serve Him, or rebel against God and suffer the consequences. Samuel was the last of the judges, the final link between two eras of Hebrew history, and he had a clear vision of God's people standing at a fork in a long road. They would either go to the right or to the left: there was no middle road. He longed for them to choose God's way, but he feared that they would not.

During the period of the judges, the Israelites had been led by men and women chosen individually by God for a specific time and purpose. God placed His Spirit upon them. Their positions were not inherited. But now the people had chosen to go the way of their neighbors; they would crown a king to rule over them. This meant attempting to establish a dynasty: the position of king would normally be inherited by sons, deserving and undeserving, from generation to generation. This choice of an earthly king to replace the rule of Yahweh through His judges posed the danger of a serious conflict for God's people. Would they put their trust in power politics, or in the divine power available through faith? The Philistine kings did exactly as they pleased, and answered to no one. But God, who had foreseen the demand for an Israelite king long ago, had laid out some basic requirements. In Deuteronomy 17:14-20, God stated that when the people should someday demand a king, that person would be of His choosing. The king must govern by God's laws, know God's Word, and follow God's commandments. The king should be an Israelite, a humble man who would not store up riches, or consider himself better than his subjects.

God chose Saul to be the first king over His people. Then God's plan for Saul's rule was put before the people. But they had a choice: both king and people might choose to follow the Lord, serving Him and obeying His commandments, or they could rebel against the Lord and go the way of the earthly monarchies.

The Power of the Covenant God (12:16-19)

Earlier in his address, Samuel had reminded the people that they had been following the Canaanite gods and had forsaken the Lord (I Sam. 12:10). When they settled into a life of agriculture, the Israelites began to look to the Canaanite fertility gods for the prosperity of their crops. But these false gods had no power to change the seasons.

Year after year the first rains fell in Palestine (as they do today) in late October and early November, softening the soil for planting. The farmers plowed and sowed their seeds while intermittent rains continued until late March. Harvesttime was from mid-April to early June—seven weeks when "rain in harvest" was as rare as "snow in summer" (Prov. 26:1).

Samuel called for the Lord to send thunder and rain during the wheat harvest—May or June—that the people might see God's power. None of the Canaanite gods had such power. And no other god would have faithfully cared for them even when they sinned.

Samuel called their rejection of God a great wickedness. The people, who considered thunder a harbinger of judgment, repented. They stood in awe in God's presence and, recognizing their sin, asked Samuel to pray for them, "that we will not die."

We might wonder why it was a sin for the people to ask for a king to rule over them. But we must remember that God's covenants with His people have always been based on trust: trust in God's Word, belief that He will do what He says He will do. In asking for a king, the people were in effect saying to God, "Even though You told us You would establish us in this land, we are losing battles. The Philistines are taking over. They have a king who fights for them. We want the same." In doing so, they rejected God's rule over them: this is always a sin.

The Affirmation (12:20-24)

The sin of the people was greater than just asking for a king to rule over them. They had rejected God and disobeyed Him in other things as well. While conquering the Canaanites, the Israelites had made treaties with pagan people, absorbing their gods and corrupt culture. For those reasons God had demanded that they separate themselves from the inhabitants of this Promised Land and live according to God's standards, in obedience to His covenant with them.

Samuel said they had "done all this evil." Yet when they repented, Samuel encouraged them. This time, he told them, follow the Lord and serve Him with all your heart. Samuel reminded them that they were chosen by God to be His very own people. God would be faithful in keeping His covenant with them.

In answer to their request for prayer, Samuel promised he would never cease to pray for them. Indeed, to stop would be to sin against the Lord. Moreover, he would continue to teach them the ways of the Lord.

God is faithful, and only He can deliver His people. Samuel was committed to prayer, considering it a sin not to pray. He was committed to teaching God's people the "good and right" way.

The Final Warning (12:25)

When Moses placed God's covenant before the Israelites centuries earlier, he closed his address with the warning that if they turned away from God they would "certainly be destroyed" (Deut. 30:18). At the end of Joshua's life, when the covenant was being renewed, Joshua warned, "If you forsake the Lord and serve foreign gods, he will turn and bring disaster on you and make an end of you, after he has been good to you" (Josh. 24:20).

The people broke the covenant, and reneged on their vows to Joshua. Now, at another renewal of the covenant, Samuel issued a warning that if the people continued in their wickedness, "both you and your king will be swept away." Like Joshua, who called for the people to "choose for yourselves this day whom you will serve (Josh. 24:15)," Samuel put the choice before the people. If they were to continue to be God's people, then both their earthly monarch and his subjects must serve and obey the heavenly King.

The words "swept away," in verse 25 come from the Latin word *consumere*, meaning "to devour, waste away, destroy, rot, reduce to ashes." The word does not seem to imply a quick action, but rather a process, a slow eating away. Consumption (a word from the same root) is a disease that causes the body to waste away. Samuel warned that if the people and their king continued in sin, their lives would be caught up in a process leading to destruction, a wasting away, until there was nothing left but ashes.

When Samuel called God's people to commit themselves to following the Lord, it was to be no halfhearted commitment. They were to make a clear choice either to serve God, obey Him, and not rebel against Him, or to forsake their God.

God's call to us today is just as clear. Jesus said, "Whosoever will come after me, let him deny himself, and take up his cross, and follow me" (Mk. 8:34b, KJV).

For Discussion:

1. What evidence do you have from your own life that God is faithful to those who serve and obey Him?

2. The Israelites were reluctant to trust God's power when they saw the earthly power of the Philistines. Do you see any parallels in our current global conflicts? What does it mean to trust God in a nuclear age?

3. The Philistines did not acknowledge God, yet gained more political power than the Israelites. Do you know people or organizations like that? What is your reaction when the wicked prosper? What is God's perspective? (See Ps. 75.)

Window on the Word

Grace and Discipleship

Cheap grace is grace without discipleship, grace without the cross, grace without Jesus Christ, living and incarnate.

Costly grace is the treasure hidden in the field, for the sake of which a man will gladly go and sell all that he has. It is the pearl of great price to buy [for] which the merchant will sell all his goods. It is the kingly rule of Christ . . . It is the call of Jesus Christ at which the disciple leaves his nets and follows him.

Costly grace is the Gospel which must be sought again and again, the gift which must be asked for, the door at which a man must knock.

Such grace is costly because it calls us to follow, and it is grace because it calls us to follow Jesus Christ. It is costly because it costs a man his life, and it is grace because it gives a man the only true life. (Dietrich Bonhoeffer, *The Cost of Discipleship*)

2

Godly Friendship

Truth to Apply: In the lives of David and Jonathan I discover the characteristics of a deep friendship rooted in God's love and purpose.

Key Verse: Jonathan became one in spirit with David, and he loved him as himself (I Sam. 18:1b).

Everyone who wants to be a friend ought to read *The Velveteen Rabbit,* by Margery Williams. It contains one of the most beautiful descriptions of love and friendship ever written—a whimsical, child's approach to life.

Two toy animals have a conversation:

"What is real?" asked the rabbit one day. "Does it mean having things that buzz inside you and a stick-out handle?"

"Real isn't how you are made," said his friend Skin Horse. "It's a thing that happens to you. When a child loves you for a long time, not just to play with, but really loves you, then you become real. It doesn't happen all at once. You become. It takes a long time. Generally by the time you become real, most of your hair has been loved off, and your eyes drop out, and you get loose in the joints and very shabby. But these things don't matter at all. Because once you are real, you can't be ugly . . . except to people who don't understand."

Do you have any friendships in which you can be truly "real"? What are the most valuable qualities of that friendship?

As the Spirit of the Lord came mightily on David, it seems that the Spirit was departing from King Saul. After winning a victory for the Israelites over the Philistines (the Goliath account), David was awarded the position of commander-in-chief over the men of war (I Sam. 18:5). Bit by bit, David was overtaking Saul's position of power in the land.

Jonathan, the other principal character in our study, was the son of Saul, and considerably older than David. When first introduced to us, Jonathan, accompanied by his armor bearer, single-handedly attacks and defeats a garrison of the enemy (I Sam. 14:1-5). He speaks as one who knows the ways of God when he boldly assures his companion that God could save "whether by many or by few" (vs. 6).

Jonathan was popular with the Israelites. We see their loyalty and love for him in the incident of their rescue of Jonathan from Saul's foolish vows (I Sam. 14:36-45).

David was profoundly influenced by Jonathan. When the latter fell on the Gilboa battlefield, it was not flattery that led him to exclaim: "Your glory, O Israel, lies slain on your heights. How the mighty have fallen!" (II Sam. 1:19). This passage of Scripture describes the initiation and development of an incredible relationship between a prince and a young shepherd—a friendship started and sealed with a covenant. Of course, this bond between Jonathan and David didn't happen immediately. It began out of Jonathan's admiration for David's military prowess, and grew deeper as they renewed their loyalty to each other in the face of severe adversity.

Light on the Text

A Friendship Sealed (18:1-4)

The writer describes Jonathan's affection for David very graphically: "Jonathan became one in spirit with David, and he loved him as himself." The Hebrew word describing their relationship (which is translated as "knit" in the KJV) denotes binding or tying something to something else. In Genesis 38:28, the midwife marked Zarah's hand by *tying* it with a scarlet thread. In Job 38:32, God reminds Job that only He *binds* the stars in place. Lives can be *bound* together in love (Gen. 44:30) or in conspiracy (I Ki. 16:9)

Jonathan loves David "as himself." What extraordinary depth of affection on Jonathan's part! The original meaning of the Hebrew word for "himself," or "his own soul," was probably "to breathe." It is translated "life" in Genesis 1:30. Jonathan, then, loved David just as he cared for his own personhood.

Their relationship was confirmed by a solemn pact, and manifested in generous gifts. Giving David his robe was more than the generous act of a king's son toward a poor shepherd boy. One writer says, "Clothing is so much a part of the person who wears it that the giving of it to another is equivalent to giving away one's own self." Jonathan, whose name means "the Lord has given," gave what best expressed the gift of himself. And he gave without any thought of getting in return. The text is silent on David's gifts, if any, to Jonathan. But to Jonathan, true friendship was apparently a commitment to *be* a friend, not just to *have* a friend.

Why was Jonathan drawn to David in such an intimate way? What did he see in David that was attractive to him? Jonathan was, as David, every inch a man. He was as dexterous with the bow as his companion was with a sling. Both men were sensitive and tender. Each man possessed a dynamic personal faith in God. Jonathan must have been encouraged when he learned how David trusted God to defeat Goliath. They had a deep interest in the well-being of God's Kingdom (I Sam. 14:6; 17:47). But someone had to take the first step toward friendship. It was Jonathan who voluntarily reached out to David. It is no coincidence that his name comes before David's in this passage. The description of Jonathan's deep affection for David recalls Jesus' answer to the question, "What is the greatest commandment?" He said the second highest law consisted in loving one's neighbor "as yourself."

A Friendship Saved (18:5—19:7)

Saul, having stooped to a new low in his wicked passion, urged his own son to become a murderer—in fact, to assassinate a dear friend. No doubt Saul pointed out to his son that David was a dangerous rival to Jonathan's own future position as king. Saul tried to play on any bit of jealousy he might find within Jonathan.

Jonathan stood at a crossroads. He faced tremendous pressure to yield to the lure of eventual wealth and power.If David were spared, Jonathan's accession to the throne would be jeopardized. Yet he had made a pact to be true and faithful no matter what the cost (18:3). Not a few have bowed to the master of self-interest, and sacrificed friendships on some wayside altar. But not Jonathan. For Jonathan, true friendship meant unconditional loyalty. He was no fair-weather friend. Even in adversity, he was committed to be a brother to David. Jonathan was truly a "friend who sticks closer than a brother" (Prov. 18:24).

Jonathan went to bat for David—at the risk of his life. Simply and gently Jonathan called the king's attention to a few facts. He first called his father's murder plot what it was: sin. He alerted Saul to what he already knew: David was innocent. He pointed out David's risks, services, approval by the Lord, and even Saul's own joy in his accomplishments. He concluded his defense with a pointed question (in effect): "Do you really think it is right to murder an innocent man?'

Jonathan won his case. Saul's heart was softened temporarily, and he made a declaration that David would be spared. Jonathan had saved David's life—and their friendship.

A Friendship Strengthened (19:8—23:29)

Certainly on this occasion Jonathan must have prayed fervently for wisdom and the best words to speak. God answered his petition. Also, Jonathan seemed to speak the truth in love. Harsh language arouses hostility, not humility. He spoke with respect, as a son to his elder. He addressed his father as "the king." In addition, he appealed to whatever remained of Saul's righteousness. Evidently at this juncture the king's heart was not so encrusted with hatred that he would murder an innocent young man.

At this point in his life, David was in a deep valley of distress. He had been hunted like an animal across Palestine's woods, deserts, and mountains. At one of his lowest ebbs, he bared his soul to Jonathan: ". . . there is only a step between me and death" (20:3). Not long afterwards he delivered a group of Israelites, but then discovered that, given the chance, they would betray him to Saul (23:1-23). Saul maintained constant pursuit of David, his men spying on his every movement, ready to report to the king any oportunity to seize him (23:14). Under such trying circumstances David must have been shackled with despair, fear, and loneliness.

Jonathan's visit and ministry of encouragement, recorded in 23:15-18, must have revived his courage and provided stamina to bear his present lot. I Samuel 23:17 illustrates how Jonathan encouraged David. He approached him from four angles:

Preservation. "My father Saul will not lay a hand on you." Jonathan might also have assured his companion, "David, if God is for you, who can be against you? (See Rom. 8:31.)

Exaltation. "You will be king over Israel." Russian novelist Dostoevski wrote, "To love a person means to see him as God intended him to be." Jonathan here helped David to visualize his potential.

Self-Renunciation. "I will be second to you." Jonathan willingly renounced his right to the throne for David's sake and in obedience to God's will. His unselfish action reminds us of John the Baptist's self-denial: "He must become greater; I must become less" (Jn. 3:30).

Information. "Even my father Saul knows this." The thrust of the original is, "Why, even Saul realizes that you will be the next king. If he believes it, David, why doubt?"

It is crucial to realize the sphere of Jonathan's encouragement. It was "in God." He was able to elevate David's thoughts from his circumstances to his God.

Is it any wonder that when Jonathan dies, David says of him, "I grieve for you, Jonathan my brother; you were very dear to me . . . ." (II Sam.1:26).

For Discussion:

1. If you knew that a friend at work was to be promoted to a position you wanted, how would you react? In what ways does envy stifle the development of our friendships?

2. Think of a time you took a risk for a friend. Perhaps the risk involved your being misunderstood, falsely accused, inconvenienced, or even betrayed. What happened? What motivated you to do this?

3. Strong bonds united David and Jonathan. What are the bonds that unite you to those close to you? Which bonds need strengthening?

Window on the Word

Self-Disclosure

In *How to Be a Friend*, by Richard P. Walters, Daniel J. Siemasko gives some valuable helps for revealing ourselves to others. He suggests the following guidelines:

Here and Now. Remember that the closer we are to the event being disclosed, both in time and personally, the more intense is the communication.

Relevant. Make sure the topic of discussion concerns both of you, not just you alone. Include your opinions about things the other person is interested in. Leave about 60 percent of the time for the other person.

Spontaneous. Don't be mechanical about it. Self-disclosure should not be a technique. It should stem from a desire to know and be known.

Controlled. Some things in our lives we don't necessarily need to share: past sins, intimate secrets, etc. Too much self-revelation is as bad as too little. Ask yourself, "Is it useful to talk about this?"

Helpful. Keep checking yourself to be sure your self-disclosure is aiding the other person. Don't expose until you know what the other person's needs are.

3

Jealousy's Bitter Roots

Truth to Apply: By studying the experience of Saul, I can understand how jealousy grows, and how it can be redirected positively.

Key Verse: Saul has slain his thousands, and David his tens of thousands (I Sam. 18:7b).

It can happen as early as the 30s; sometimes it doesn't happen till the 60s. But it usually happens in the 40s or 50s. It can happen to men or women, rich or poor, educated or not. And it's no fun.

What is it? It's a common condition we call the "if onlies." At some point in middle adulthood, something happens to make people analyze their lives. The last child leaves home. The last promotion is reached at work. A parent dies or becomes dependent on the children.

At such a time, the adult may ask himself or herself questions like these: What have I really accomplished in my life? What can I look forward to? What impact has my life had on other people? What have I done well?

Such questions can lead to "if only" feelings like these: remorse ("If only I hadn't done that"); recrimination ("If only they hadn't done that to me"); regret ("If only things had happened differently"). For some people, the "if onlies" can lead to bitterness toward self and others, or resentment and jealousy—especially toward younger people. These feelings often play a big role in what is usually called mid-life crisis.

What is your experience with jealousy, or the "if onlies"? What are the feelings involved? How do you deal with them?

Saul had a good start as king. He was attractive, the people liked him, and he soon had an impressive military victory to his credit (I Sam. 10—12). But I Samuel 13 describes his first mistake.

Fresh from a victory over a Philistine garrison, Saul went to Gilgal and summoned volunteers from all Israel to join his army. Meanwhile, the Philistines arrived in force for a counterattack. Samuel had promised to come in seven days to offer sacrifices and ask for God's help in the battle. But the appointed time passed and Samuel still had not appeared. The frightened volunteers started going home, or even fleeing the country. In a desperate attempt to save the situation, Saul offered the sacrifice himself—which indicated a radical lack of faith in God and a presumptuous assessment of his own significance.

The altar was still warm when Samuel showed up and delivered a stinging message from God: "But now your kindgom will not endure; the Lord has sought out a man after his own heart" (I Sam. 13:14).

The disobedience of Saul's heart was confirmed in a later incident, as was God's judgment: "Because you have rejected the word of the Lord, he has rejected you as king" (I Sam. 15:23).

Chapter 16 describes the anointing of David as king, and the beginning of his career. From this point on, Saul traveled a downhill trail. David, however, was God's chosen. And Saul knew it.

Light on the Text

Competence (18:5)

Shortly after David's anointing (16:13), Saul became tormented by "an evil spirit from the Lord" (16:14). The effect of this visitation was a deep depression, perhaps even dread, that could be lifted only temporarily through skillfully played music. One of Saul's servants recommended David, and the young shepherd soon became a frequent visitor to the palace (16:14-23).

After David defeated Goliath (chap. 17), what had been a temporary assignment (17:15) became permanent (18:2). David became a resident of the palace, and a close friendship developed between David and Saul's son, Jonathan (18:1-4).

Such rapid promotion spells ruin for many people. The limelight soon exposes glaring cracks in the apparently perfect facade. But David was different. He was a man of integrity. The image he presented to the world was an accurate reflection of his character. Under the closest scrutiny and the toughest conditions, he showed his true worth. And people liked what they saw.

Comparison (18:6, 7)

We don't know how long the war with the Philistines lasted, but the events in these verses probably took place at the end of the war which began with Goliath's death.

Upon the return of the victorious Israelites, there was a spontaneous national celebration. The women met the returning soldiers with impromptu songs of praise and dancing. These women were probably performing dances that mimicked the victory. As they danced, they sang in alternating choruses, one chorus answering another. In the choruses, David and Saul were compared—to Saul's disadvantage—and Saul didn't like it one bit!

Complaint (18:8, 9)

The fact that Saul could feel threatened by a young shepherd like David shows how far Saul had sunk. The impressive-looking young man described in I Samuel 9:2 had become a brooding, frightened, suspicious man, old before his time. Saul had lost his objectivity. Instead of admitting his responsibility for his condition and seeking healing in God's forgiveness, he tried frantically to hold on to his position by eliminating likely contenders, specifically David. From that day forward, much of Saul's time and energy was diverted from his kingly duties to a growing obsession with David.

How should Saul have reacted to the praise David was getting? Most leaders would probably take such praise to be a compliment of their ability to choose highly skilled subordinates. This should have been especially true in David's case, since David wasn't trying to gain glory for himself. He was simply serving Saul.

Conflict (18:10, 11)

At first, music was able to soothe Saul's depression and melancholy. But after a while Saul began to lose control. At its very root, Saul's problem was spiritual: the Spirit of the Lord had left him (16:14). The apostle Paul, in Romans 1:24-32, mentions several ways God gave people up to follow their own selfish, sinful desires. Saul's appears to be such a case. When the restraining Spirit of God was removed, Saul was wide open to evil influence. His inclination toward the occult is revealed later when he consults a spiritist medium (I Sam. 28:7ff).

As had happened before, David was summoned to play his harp. Saul may have been holding the javelin like a scepter—a fitting symbol of office for a military king. So "hurled" may mean "swung"—an attempt to pin David to the wall by a spear thrust.

Consequences (18:12-16)

Since Saul's problems were within himself, sending David out of his sight didn't help. Before long, Saul was getting glowing reports of David's successes and his popularity with everyone (see 18:5). As commander of 1,000 soldiers, David conducted many military campaigns and performed so well that Saul was forced to honor him. However, there is no hint that David ever tried to blow his own horn and steal people's affections away from Saul. On the contrary, David acted conscientiously and enthusiastically on Saul's behalf.

From Saul's example, it is evident that jealousy destroys the person who indulges in it. Sometimes it can destroy others, too. Though Saul wasn't successful in destroying David, he certainly made things difficult for him. But notice that David avoided the traps of resentment and revenge. He remained faithful to the Lord, and prospered as Saul declined.

Other Examples

Saul is not a unique case. The Bible gives us many examples of jealousy. The chart below lists some of the more well-known Biblical jealousies:

Passage	Who was involved	What caused the jealousy?	What were the effects?
Gen. 4:3-8	Cain and Abel.	A rejected sacrifice.	Cain murdered Abel.
Gen. 37:4-11	Joseph and his brothers.	Joseph was their father's favorite; he told his brothers that he'd dreamed about being over them.	Joseph's brothers sold him into slavery, but God raised him to a position of power that enabled him to save the lives of his family members.
Dan. 6:3, 4	Daniel and the other rulers under Darius.	Daniel was doing an excellent job, and Darius planned to promote him.	The other rulers convinced Darius to make a law that Daniel couldn't obey in good conscience. God spared Daniel from the lions, and the plotters were eaten instead.
Acts 13:44-50	Paul and Barnabas and the Jews.	Paul and Barnabas attracting large crowds with their preaching.	The Jews had them chased out of town—a persecution that continued throughout the trip. But this had the effect of helping the Gospel spread far and fast.
Phil. 1:12-18	Paul and other preachers of the Gospel.	Others wanted a piece of Paul's success.	The Gospel was spread even further.

For Discussion:

1. Someone has said that envy is wanting something someone else has; jealousy is fear that something you have will be taken away. What did Saul fear would be taken away from him? Were his fears well founded? How might he have handled his fears?

2. Has anyone ever said they were jealous of you? If so, how did you deal with their feelings?

3. How might you help people who are jealous of you gain a proper perspective?

Window on the Word

Bragging About Gifts

What bothers me . . . is a "look at me" attitude when it comes to spiritual gifts. "Bless God, I've got it!" (With the unspoken questions: Why don't *you* have it? Don't you wish you did?)

We seem to delight in parading our gifts, forgetting the God who gave them to us. I have heard people compare their spiritual experiences. Those without similar experiences are properly awed and put down. They are made to feel like second-class citizens of the Kingdom of God, and they worry about not having what the others have.

The show-off forgets three things. First, that God gave the gifts. Second, that we do not need to be good or spiritual or righteous or deserving to receive gifts. Third, that a father gives different gifts to different children, according to their needs and the results he wants to accomplish in their lives.

Take, for instance, an evergreen tree. There it sits in the middle of the forest, doing its thing. One day a woodchopper comes along, cuts the tree down, and puts it on a truck. The tree is placed on a lot, bought, taken to a home, and finally decorated.

Suppose that the tree, looking down at the twinkling lights, the gaily colored ornaments, the shining tinsel, says to itself, "Look at me! I'm really something!" Wouldn't that be ridiculous? Wouldn't we say to the tree, "You fool! You did not decorate yourself. Those gifts were placed upon you for a purpose, and when there is no need for them they will be removed by those who put them there." (John Sterner, *How to Become Super-Spiritual [or Kill Yourself Trying]*)

4

When God Calls, Listen!

Truth to Apply: Just as God called David to be a leader of his people, I am called to discover how I can "shepherd" others.

Key Verse: I took you from the pasture and from following the flock to be ruler over my people Israel (II Sam. 7:8b).

Four-year-old Bryan stood with his father at one end of a long plank bridging a muddy spot between them and the playground swings. Looking at the narrow board, Bryan clutched at his father's legs. "Please hold me, Daddy," he begged. "I'm afraid."

Taking Bryan's grubby fist firmly, his father replied, "Don't be afraid. I will walk with you." And he led Bryan safely to the other side.

The next day as Bryan was playing with two-year-old Jeremy, his mother heard him say, "This is a bridge over the mud. Let's walk across it." Peering into the playroom, she saw a board laid on the floor, both boys at one end. "Don't be afraid," said Bryan, as Jeremy hung back. He grabbed Jeremy's hand. "I will walk with you."

Bryan had taken a big step in the process of growing up. Having been helped himself, he was ready to help someone else with the same need.

Has anyone ever "shepherded" you? At this point in your life, what is the potential for you to become a shepherd to someone else?

Background/Overview: *II Samuel 5:1-3; 7:8-16*

David's reign began about 1010 B.C., and lasted for 40 years, seven in his first capital at Hebron, and 33 in Jerusalem (I Ki. 2:11). His coronation over all Israel marked the nation's rise into world prominence. David had overcome the threat of the Philistines. Thus God's people were relatively free to expand and develop; there were no major external threats to their security. For a while, less than 80 years, Israel was one of the great nations of its day.

Internally, however, David needed to consolidate the kingdom. When Saul died, the southern two tribes of Judah and Benjamin recognized David as their king (II Sam 2:4). The ten northern tribes, however, under Saul's captain, Abner, had put Saul's son Ish-Bosheth on the throne (II Sam. 2:8-10).

Civil war ensued (II Sam. 3:6), ended only by the treacherous slaying of Abner by Joab (David's captain), and of Ish-Bosheth by two of his own subordinates (II Sam. 3:27; 4:5-7). Thus leaderless, the elders of Israel sought out David.

Light on the Text

The Shepherd's Foundation (5:1-3)

God chose David to be king even before the death of Saul (I Sam. 16:12). Yet David had to make some strategic moves in order to win the loyalty of the ten northern tribes of Israel, who for some time had given their allegiance to Saul's son, Ish-Bosheth (II Sam. 2:8-10).

As king of the southern tribes, David chose as his capital the historic city of Hebron, 20 miles south of Jerusalem. Later, recognizing the hostility between the north and south, he forestalled charges of favoritism by moving his capital to what amounted to neutral territory—the Jebusite city of Jerusalem. By conquering the as-yet-unconquered stronghold, he made this city into crown property.

It must have been humbling for the northern tribes to have to acknowledge David as king. But nobody forced them to this decision. They chose him deliberately, possibly with a nod to political expediency—there were no other contenders. Also, they had undoubtedly observed Judah's prosperity under David during the seven and a half years of his reign (vs. 5). A number of other reasons probably figured into their choice. They were aware of David's leadership qualities (vs. 2). He was a proven military leader who also handled political situations tactfully and firmly. And he was popular with the people: "everything the king did pleased them" (II Sam. 3:36).

Finally, David satisfied the requirements for kingship on two counts. He was an Israelite (Deut. 17:15), and he had been anointed by Samuel (I Sam. 16:12, 13).

So David made a compact, or contract, with Israel. This type of formal declaration was made when a new dynasty came into power. When the contract had been ratified, the religious ceremony took place (vs. 3). In noting that the pledge had been made before the Lord, the king was anointed with oil, which "signified the consecration to an office in the theocracy" (*The International Standard Bible Encyclopedia*). David showed great skill as a military and political leader, and wisdom in handling people. Beyond that, he was also patient, generous, and faithful. David had waited long years to be king, yet without becoming bitter. He had remained faithful to Saul, the Lord's anointed, even while Saul tried to kill him. He had displayed generosity in his dealings with Abner, and now again with the leaders of the ten tribes.

The Shepherd's Function (7:8-11a)

When David expressed a desire to build a house for the Lord (7:1-3), the prophet Nathan's immediate human reaction was "Great!" But God sent His final decision through Nathan to David, postponing the building of a temple.

The text here is written in poetic form, phrase repeating phrase for emphasis. It starts with a confirmation of divine will: "Thus saith the Lord." These are Nathan's credentials: he is not making his own private judgment, as he had the day before, but is passing on God's official verdict to David.

First God set up a new relationship with David (vs. 8). Then God reviewed what He had done for David (vs. 9), pointing out that support, victory, and fame were all gifts from Him:

(1) God had been with David constantly, in companionship and in supportive presence. Doubtless David had already sensed this (I Sam. 17:37, 45; 18:14); he had known God beside him all the way.

(2) God had given David success: He had "cut off" David's enemies (see I Sam. 23:5; 30:17, 18).

(3) God was giving David recognition. Even in his late thirties (5:4), David's name was becoming as well known as "the name of the great men that are in the earth"— names from history (like Abraham and Moses), from the contemporary setting (as Hiram of Tyre), and from the future, for "later ages were to look back to him as an ideal and also look forward in type to a new David, an anointed one, a Messiah" (Peter Ackroyd, *The Cambridge Bible Commentary: The Second Book of Samuel*).

Finally, in this portion of Scripture, God promised David three blessings for His people: a place, permanence, and peace (vs.10). God repeated the pledge He made to Abraham (Gen. 12:1-3) for a home for "my people Israel." No longer nomadic, having conquered the area under Joshua and developed a primitive government with the judges, Israel was now ready to settle down into the Promised Land as God's own people, His chosen ones.

The permanence of this settlement is shown in the image used: God would "plant" Israel, like a vine; Israel would "have a place of their own." Peace was also promised. No longer would Israel's enemies, especially the warlike Philistines, molest them. They would have respite, freedom from the conflict they had had in the past.

The Shepherd's Future (7:11b-16)

These verses open with a confirmation of their source: the message was not coming from Nathan's imagination but "the Lord declares to you." God promised to establish David's dynasty, his dream, his son's throne, and his son's relationship with God forever.

First, God established David's line of succession. There are two lists of David's sons. One list (II Sam.3:2-5; 5:14-16) names 17; the parallel passage (I Chr. 3:1-9) gives 19. In both, Solomon is listed as the tenth born, fourth after his father's rise to the throne. As with David himself (the youngest son), God bypassed the usual system of succession in favor of Solomon. The far-reaching implications of this promise to David's seed are found in the coming of Christ, in David's lineage.

Second, David's dream of building a temple for the Lord would also be realized through Solomon (vss. 2, 13). Since all of David's foes had not yet been conquered, David could not build the Temple, but with "rest on every side," the proper time would come (I Ki. 5:2-5). It was not appropriate that David, a man of war, should build the Temple, in which worship pointed to the Prince of Peace.

Third, new relationships would also be established by God through Solomon. The father/son concept is mentioned, an idea developed later. Hebrews picks up this verse in reference to Christ (Heb. 1:5).

Finally, David's throne was to be permanent (vss. 11, 13, 16). Whether referred to as a "house" (descendants), a "kingdom" (rule, or authority), or a "throne" (seat of power), the relationship was to be "forever" (fulfilled throught Jesus Christ).

Consider the wide variety of backgrounds of people God called to some special ministry. How did each one's background contribute to later service to God?

Moses: Shepherd, Ex. 3:1-12
Daniel: Civil servant, Dan. 1:4-6, 17
Peter: Fisherman, Mt. 4:18-22
Matthew: Herod's IRS man, Mt. 9:9
Luke: Medical doctor, Col. 4:14
Paul: Tentmaker, Acts 18:3
Mary: Housekeeper, Luke 10:38-42
Lydia: Merchandiser, Acts 16:14, 15

Make a brief survey of your own occupation, talents, training and education, abilities, family situation, to evaluate what preparation you have had for offering your services to God. Think about what opportunities could grow out of your own background.

For Discussion

1. How did David use the experiences and character traits of his early years as leader of God's flock?

2. David developed leadership qualities by faithfully doing what might be considered "menial" work. What can you learn from certain jobs that you feel are beneath you?

Window on the Word

The Shepherd

I do not remember ever having seen in the East a flock of sheep without a shepherd. In such a landscape as Judea, where a day's pasture is thinly scattered over an unfenced tract of country, covered with delusive paths, still frequented by wild beasts, and rolling off into the desert, the man and his character are indispensable. On some high moor, across which at night the hyenas howl, when you meet him, sleepless, farsighted, weather-beaten, armed, leaning upon his staff, and looking out over the scattered sheep, every one of them on his heart, you understand why the shepherd of Judea sprang to the front in his people's history; why they gave his name to their king, and made him the symbol of providence; why Christ took him as the type of self-sacrifice. (George Adam Smith, *The Historical Geography of the Holy Land*)

5

Rebellion and Reconciliation

Truth to Apply: The example of Absalom's rebellion can motivate me to find opportunities for reconciliation with loved ones.

Key Verse: So [Absalom] stole the hearts of the men of Israel (II Sam. 15:6b).

Situation: John, a high school graduating senior, has left home following an argument with his father. He is now living with a close friend down the street. "Why should I go to John's graduation?" says John's father. "No one asked him to leave home, and I'm not going to give him the satisfaction of thinking he's right and I'm wrong."

Situation: Judy, the Bradleys' 15-year-old daughter, is pregnant. She has rebelled against everything her parents stand for: their faith in God, their values, their life-style. When told of the pregnancy, the parents send Judy to her room, and then discuss it. "We'll send Judy to her aunt's in New York," says her mother. "Obviously she can't stay here. I won't have our family gossiped about. I just couldn't stand the talk in this town."

Situation: Tom, with three friends, has been picked up by the police for drug possession. They are being held in jail. Tom's father has just been notified. "The situation is out of my hands," he says. "I can't help Tom. Maybe the police can. He knows I love him, but nothing I say gets through to him. I'll pay for his lawyer, but there's no point in my going to see Tom."

Some children may choose to walk down a different path from their parents, rejecting love and guidance. The children in the cases above are not blameless. But what are the attitudes of the parents that hinder the beginnings of reconciliation?

Background/Overview: *II Samuel 15:2-12*

God forgave David's sin of taking Bathsheba, the wife of Uriah the Hittite, but warned him that the sword would never depart from his house (II Sam. 12:10). How true this was. David loved his children, but there was continual strife in his household.

Absalom's rebellion against his father took root when David's eldest son, Amnon, raped Tamar, his half sister. The dejected young woman was taken into the household of Absalom, her brother. When David did not punish Amnon, Absalom spent two years plotting revenge for the crime against his sister. Finally, he invited all his brothers to a feast and had Amnon killed. Absalom was then forced to flee to Geshur for refuge in the home of Talmai, his grandfather. He remained there in exile for three years.

We are told that "the spirit of the king longed to go to Absalom," but he took no action to bring Absalom home. It was not until Joab sent a woman to King David to plead the case of her exiled son that David recognized the similarity to his own story. He brought Absalom home, but did not allow Absalom to come into his presence for two years. During this time, Absalom's heart festered with resentment against his father.

Angry because Joab also had ignored him, Absalom burned Joab's barley fields. This commanded Joab's attention, and he then served as mediator between David and Absalom. Father and son were now brought together, but it was much too late. The conspiracy was well advanced; Absalom had already rejected his father.

Light on the Text

The Rebellious Son (15:2-6)

Like David in his youth, Absalom was a handsome man. He was praised "for his handsome appearance," and "from the top of his head to the sole of his foot there was no blemish in him" (II Sam. 14:25). He was a natural leader and a family man with three sons and one daughter. All these characteristics appeared to make him a likely candidate for the throne.

Still, Absalom wanted to make sure of his ascension. He arranged for chariots, horses, and 50 men to run before him as he entered the city gate early each morning (II Sam. 15:1). He staged a royal arrival that marked him as a man bidding for the throne.

Once at the gate, Absalom played the role of popular politician. He ignored the forms of submission to royalty and tried to establish a sense of equality among citizens. He called out greetings to people as they came through the gate, and inquired about their welfare. Then when they could not find a judge to hear their complaints, Absalom seized the opportunity to point out the problems of King David's government. The crafty prince suggested that if he were judge, he would personally see that everyone was served justice.

Absalom's promises sounded good, but they were deceitful. He won the people over by feigning compassion and humanitarianism—qualities he did not possess. He also made promises that he could never fulfill. He was a man who used whatever he could to gain what he wanted.

Notice the progression of Absalom's deceit through these verses as he attempts to win the hearts of the people. First, Absalom made himself available to the people. He got up early and waited by the gate. He listened as people came in asking for the king, and then he called out a greeting. "Where are you from, friends? I see you are strangers. Can I help you?"

Next, he pointed out the faults in the existing judicial system and suggested that, given a chance, he would correct them. Absalom explained that neither the king nor his deputy were at the gate. When the people showed indignation at this, Absalom offered sympathy. He remarked that he would handle matters in a much better way if he were in charge.

Last, he put himself on the people's level. He shook their hands, embraced them, and kissed them—forms of personal greeting in the Near East.

Absalom's Lies (15:7-9)

After four years Absalom was ready to bring his plan (to usurp the throne) out into the open. He chose Hebron as the place to make his announcement. The highest town in Palestine, Hebron was 19 miles south of Jerusalem, and a seat of Jewish history. Here Abraham and Sarah, Isaac and Rebekah, Jacob and Leah, and all of Jacob's sons with the exception of Joseph, were buried. Here, too, David had been anointed king of Judah and, later, king of Israel. Hebron remained David's capital for seven and one-half years; and when he moved the government north, the Judeans were not pleased. With seeds of discontent already planted and growing, Absalom decided Hebron was the place to raise the standard of rebellion against his father.

But David knew none of Absalom's thoughts. While living in Jerusalem, Absalom must have appeared to be a good son. He seemed to be taking an interest in the people and the government.

Note Absalom's humble manner as he approached his father to ask permission to go to Hebron. "I pray thee, let me go . . ." (KJV). He presented a picture of a pious young man who wanted to fulfill a vow he had made to the Lord. The vow, he said, was made during the time he was with his grandfather in exile at Geshur. David was deceived by Absalom's lies. How could he deny such a request? "Go in peace," David said. So Absalom left his father and went to Hebron.

Absalom's Tragic Conspiracy (15:10-12)

At this point, Absalom's plot was moving toward a climax. A network of spies had been working for several years, undermining confidence in King David and preparing the way for Absalom to take over.

Verse 10 suggests a note of expectancy. Runners preceded the royal entourage saying, "Listen for the sound of the trumpet! When you hear it, Absalom will reign in Hebron." The trumpet was used to bring news to the people and was a customary means of announcing the crowning of a king. (See I Ki. 1:39 and II Ki. 9:13 for examples.) Absalom's entourage must have been a stately group. His carriage and 50 horsemen were joined by 200 invited guests from Jerusalem. These were no doubt prominent men with leadership positions in Jerusalem. In his deceit, Absalom involved them in the conspiracy by lying about the purpose of the trip. Had they known the truth, they probably would not have gone.

This was not the first time Absalom had deceived guests. Several years earlier he had invited all the king's sons to a sheepshearing, a day of feasting and merriment. But Absalom's real plan was to kill Amnon, his brother (II Sam. 13:23-29). The guests of this second intrigue were different, but the heart of Absalom was the same. He needed them to make his journey look authentic to his father.

He used another of David's companions as well, this one a trusted counselor in the court. Ahithophel was possibly the grandfather of Bathsheba, and so it is possible that he joined the revolt to avenge the disgrace of his family. Absalom must have recognized his attitude, whereas David did not. Reaching into the inner circle of his father's friends, Absalom's conspiracy was all the more bitter. Added to this group were a growing number of people throughout the kingdom.

David was apparently blind to the conspiracy. Why? One reason could be that David rarely saw Absalom. We know that he was banished from his father's presence for several years, and had lived in Jerusalem without seeing David for two years (II Sam. 14:28). No doubt reports of his son's activities came to David, but as a loving father, he denied that his son could plot against him. In the presence of his father, Absalom probably appeared a dutiful, humble son.

The people from Jerusalem must have seen Absalom in the same way. They believed him implicitly, never doubting that he was telling them the truth. But their relationship with Absalom was one-sided. They trusted Absalom; he betrayed their trust and used them to his advantage.

David loved his son Absalom. Why did he not seek reconciliation? Probably for many of the same reasons parents today find it difficult to take steps to be reconciled with their children. Yet God always expects His people to work toward reconciliation. He has set an

example by continually calling His own rebellious
children back to Himself.

For Discussion

1. What experiences have you had in which pride was a
hindrance to reconciliation? What steps could you take
now to start on the path of reconciliation?

2. Most of us have experienced times of rebellion in our
own lives, against parents, authority figures, God. What
were the factors that helped bring about a changed
heart? What hindered the process of repentance?

3. What help is there, among Christians, for those who
have been rejected by their children?

Window on the Word

Parenting Expert?

A young student of child behavior frequently delivered a
lecture called "Ten Commandments for Parents." He
married and became a father. The title of the lecture was
changed to "Ten Hints for Parents." Another child
arrived. The lecture became "Some Suggestions for
Parents." A third child was born. The lecturer stopped
lecturing.

6

In Tune with God

Truth to Apply: With God's help I can grow in my capacity to be sensitive to others.

Key Verses: I am going to tear the kingdom out of Solomon's hand and give you ten tribes. I will do this because they have forsaken me (I Kings 11:31b, 33a).

It had been a bravura performance. After the encore, the guitarist took a final bow and came offstage.

A young reporter waited in the musician's dressing room. He was astounded by the grace and sensitivity with which the guitarist played. He stood up as the guitarist entered the room.

"Simply brilliant. How do you make it seem like your guitar sings?"

The guitarist sat down. "It's like anything else in life. You need to have sensitivity to deal effectively with a situation, a person, and in my case, with my guitar.

"These calluses on the fingertips of my left hand prove my sensitivity toward my instrument. It cost me some pain to be a sensitive musician.

"The calluses," the guitarist said, holding up his left hand, "have not really made me insensitive to pain. Oh, my fingertips don't hurt anymore when I play—but the calluses are reminders. Reminders of the pain I went through to become sensitive toward my instrument. The practicing hurt. But past the pain was great satisfaction."

Becoming sensitive toward others is not a painless process. Indeed, much of our sensitivity can be measured by how we perceive the "calluses" we have developed over the years. They can be used to make music, or they can simply bear witness to some degree of present insensitivity. What is your experience with the calluses of life?

Background/Overview: *I Kings 11:26-33; 12:15, 16*

Throughout this Scripture portion, mention is made of the conscriptive labor force Solomon drafted out of his kingdom (I Ki. 5:13). The technical word for such a force is *corvée* (cor-VAY). A corvée implies the following conditions:

1) Work to benefit the public or government is being done.

2) The government is "drafting" workers out of the population, much like a military draft.

3) The laborers are unpaid or partially paid.

Solomon's corvée was only used on certain projects. Corvée workers were not exposed to the brutal conditions of the renowned mines of Solomon, for instance (I Ki. 8:20-22). Slaves from conquered nations were the mine workers.

The fact that they were not working the mines was little comfort to Solomon's corvée workers, however. Their self-determination was being taken away. The lack of pay seemed to prove that they were being counted as little more than slaves in the eyes of their ruler. When this was combined with steep taxes, Solomon's subjects were ready for a change in leadership.

Light on the Text

A Prophet's Illustration (11:26-31)

Solomon's kingdom faced a fiscal crisis. David had been able to fund projects out of plunder from conquered peoples. Solomon had no peoples left to conquer, so his funds had to come from a different source.

Solomon had worked to build his nation's trade revenues through some delicate political maneuvers. But those revenues had not been enough to keep up with expenses, much less the expansion of his building projects. In an attempt to keep up with costs, Solomon decreed that each of the kingdom's 12 administrative districts would be responsible for one month's court provisions. Considering what is listed as one day's provisions (I Ki. 4:22, 23), this would have been a severe strain on the resources of some of the poorer districts.

Still the financial crisis persisted. At this point Solomon instituted a plan to force freeborn Israelites to work for no pay. You can imagine how unpopular this was! The economy was in such extreme danger that Solomon signed over cities from his kingdom to the king of Tyre (I Ki. 9:10-14)!

Two citizens, Ahijah and Jeroboam, became aware of the king's desperation. They met privately outside of Jerusalem in a field. Ahijah, a prophet from Shiloh, wore a new garment to the meeting to illustrate the prophecy he gave. He took the new garment from his body and tore it into 12 pieces. He then gave Jeroboam ten of the pieces.

Jeroboam was a labor gang boss responsible for the work done by the "house of Joseph" (I Ki. 11:28). By all appearances, he did not enjoy his job. I Kings 11:27, 28 indicates that his reason for rebelling against Solomon was his own experience with the kingdom's forced labor projects. Jeroboam was a man caught in between, it seems. Although he was appointed to lead a forced labor gang, he probably shared the sentiments of the freeborn Israelites.

Ahijah declared that, indeed, it would be an act of God when the kingdom was torn from Solomon. But the handing of ten pieces of the garment to Jeroboam indicated that the new leader had already been chosen. It was only a matter of time.

A Wise Man's Folly (11:32, 33)

Solomon and his successors were left with one tribe (Benjamin) along with their own tribe, Judah. (You will recall that Saul was out of Benjamin. So the tribes from which Israel's first three kings had come were about to be separated from the rest of the nation.) Ahijah minced no words about the cause of God's judgment on Solomon's kingdom. From a prophetic perspective, Solomon's insensitivity had allowed a grand-scale desertion from the God of Israel in his kingdom.

In the ancient Near East, it was common practice for kingdoms to seal trade and political alliances with royal marriages. As Solomon worked to make his kingdom and his personal life-style more cosmopolitan, alliances and marriages ensued. Not wishing to offend the religious sensibilities of new political partners (or wives, for that matter), Solomon encouraged the building of shrines and temples to their deities in his kingdom. As time went on, he even joined them in their worship (I Ki. 11:1-8). Such blatant idolatry was a clear compromise of Solomon's heritage (I Ki. 11:9-13). The compromise would cost Solomon his kingdom. The man often thought of as the wisest in history had lost his sensitivity toward his subjects.

A King's Insensitivity (12:15)

Solomon, having heard of Jeroboam's potential for rebellion, had Jeroboam driven out of Israel. Jeroboam took refuge in Egypt until Solomon's death. Then Solomon's son Rehoboam succeeded his father to the throne.

Rehoboam had been raised entirely in the luxury of the royal court, sheltered from life outside the royal context. So Rehoboam's own sensitivity to his subjects suffered in part from his background.

Rehoboam's ability to deal with the national fiscal crisis was untested. But with the new ruler came the possibility of a change from oppressive taxes and forced labor. So the people asked Rehoboam to ease their burden, promising their loyalty in return (I Ki. 12:1-4). Rehoboam promised an answer in three days (12:5).

Rehoboam consulted two generations of court advisers. The older generation, men who had served under Solomon, had seen the forced labor and high taxes drain the patience of the people. If the kingdom were to be held together, they advised, the people's request should be carefully considered. Rehoboam should deal gently with his subjects, they said (12:6, 7).

But the younger generation of advisers had different counsel. This generation of counselors had grown up with Rehoboam in the luxury of the royal court. They shared his sheltered perspective and seemed to be most concerned that Rehoboam take a firm stand as ruler of the people. Their advice to Rehoboam proved that they shared his insensitivity. The counsel to deal harshly with the people would prove to be the undoing of the kingdom: the promise of harsher treatment under already intolerable conditions confirmed the people's worst fears (12:12-14). Scripture puts it succinctly: "the king did not listen to the people." It appears that Rehoboam gave token consideration at best to his people's request. He effectually said, "The royal person is the only concern of the kingdom. You are simply at my disposal." Ahijah's prophecy was about to be fulfilled.

A Nation's Disintegration (12:16)

The people's hopes had been pinned on Rehoboam's dealing humanely with them. But his response to their request dashed their hopes. They had not come to Rehoboam unprepared, however. Jeroboam was among the interested listeners to Rehoboam's response. Ahijah's prophecy had given him a vested interest in the situation. Jeroboam's very presence indicates at least some anticipation of what Rehoboam might say.

It had been hard enough for some of the people to accept the very idea of a united monarchy. Tribal loyalties still ran strong. The perceived need of the monarchy to consolidate national power under itself had been a consistent source of tension between the king and the people. As kings felt less need to court their subjects' support, their skill at dealing sensitively with their subjects diminished. When the monarchy achieved consolidation of power under itself, the skill seemed to disappear altogether.

It is little wonder, then, that the people felt alienated from the monarchy. Perhaps they even felt betrayed. Tribal government guaranteed a hearing of concerns by someone who was somehow related. A king could only come from one tribe.

The rhetorical question of I Kings 12:16, brought by ten tribes of the nation, crystallized their feelings of alienation: "What share do we have in David?" The insensitivity of the monarchy toward the people was convincing the people that the answer to the question was, "None." Ten tribes of the kingdom seceded from the nation: "Look after your own house, O David." The years of insensitivity brought division to the kingdom, according to the prophet's words.

For Discussion

1. In your opinion, what life experiences and habits might cause someone to develop insensitivity?

2. Recall persons who have been sensitive to your needs. What actions and attitudes proved their sensitivity to you?

3. Has anyone called your attention to an area of insensitivity to God or to others? If so, what are practical steps you can take to develop sensitivity?

Window on the Word

Light Sensitive

Beyond the complicated chemical processes that involve developers, rinses, and washes, photography depends upon a very simple circumstance: light's ability to leave an impression on film. Skilled photographers can use many different filters and lens settings, but it all boils down to that very simple characteristic of light.

Suppose for a moment that cardboard was in the camera instead of film. The light could hit the cardboard through the camera lens again and again. Maybe after a few years of such exposure, the cardboard would begin to fade in one spot. But the result wouldn't be anything like a photograph! So we come to a second very simple circumstance upon which the art of photography depends: the ability of the film to receive light.

If the substance in the camera is light sensitive, the light can make an impression on it, and that substance can then give a picture of what the light revealed.

Our sensitivity to God's light determines how accurately we can portray His light to others.

7

No Competitors

Truth to Apply: I am challenged by the example of Elijah to serve God with my whole heart.

Key Verse: How long will you waver between two opinions? If the Lord is God, follow him; but if Baal is God, follow him (I Kings 18:21).

We generally think of competition as a good thing. Consider the breakup of Bell Telephone, for example. The theory behind it was that as more companies were allowed to "fight it out" in the marketplace, the prices for telephone service would go down and the quality would go up.

Whether the theory has worked is yet to be seen. But the breakup forced people to ask a lot of questions they rarely asked before, like, "Which company is really best? Should I stay with the old familiar way of 'reaching out and touching someone'? Or should I try another company? How do I make a decision?"

Competition raises questions that may never have been asked before. Perhaps that's why the people of Israel became confused when the followers of the gods of Baal began to compete for the Israelites' allegiance. "We know Jehovah," the Hebrews must have thought, "but what about these new gods? Would they be stronger and serve our needs better? How can we find out?"

But the God of the universe allows no competitors! No other gods can hold a candle to the Lord God. King Ahab and his subjects had to learn this the hard way.

What is God's strongest competitor for *your* loyalty?

Background/Overview: *I Kings 16:30—18:39*

The rebellion of the northern tribes under Jeroboam, set in motion an unfortunate train of events. To keep the people of his new kingdom at home, Jeroboam built places of worship at Bethel and Dan. Thus he kept his subjects away from the sanctuary in Jerusalem, and led them into idolatry.

Because of Jeroboam's sin, God used Baasha to overthrow Jeroboam's son Nadab, and to destroy all of Jeroboam's descendants (I Ki. 14:9-11; 15:25-30). Baasha ruled for over 20 years, but his dynasty, too, was short-lived. His son Elah was assassinated by an army officer name Zimri (I Ki. 16:8-10). More bloodshed followed when Omri, the commander of the army, moved quickly against Zimri, forcing him to commit suicide (I Ki. 16:15-18). During Omri's rule and that of his son Ahab, the Northern Kingdom reached a level of importance and achievement it had not known before.

Under the influence of the Phenician princess Jezebel, whom he married for political reasons, Ahab began to use funds from the royal treasury to support the cult of Baal. As a result his capital city, Samaria, which had been built by his father, became a center of idolatry.

Light on the Text

Spiritual Lapse in the Royal House (16:30-33)

When Ahab assumed the throne in Samaria, Jeroboam had been dead for about 25 years. But Ahab did nothing to reverse the policies of Jeroboam that had led to Israel's spiritual decline.

Ahab ordered a temple built for Baal in Samaria, thus giving official status to Baal worship. He put an altar for Baal in a prominent place in this temple.

Who exactly was "Baal"? *The New Westminster Dictionary of the Bible* explains: "Baal worship apparently had its origin in the belief that every tract of ground owed its productivity to a supernatural being, or *baal*, that dwelt there. The farmers probably thought that from the Baals, or fertility gods, of various regions came the increase of crops, fruits, and cattle. In the Ugaritic literature, Baal seems identical with the storm-god Hadad."

The worship of Baal was often linked with that of the goddess Asherah, and the use of the Asherah pole. This pole is what the KJV is referring to when it says that Ahab made "a grove."

Elijah Lays Down Yahweh's Challenge (18:17-21)

Fearful judgment came on the land. Out of nowhere, the prophet Elijah appeared before Ahab to tell him, "As the Lord, the God of Israel, lives, whom I serve, there will be neither dew nor rain in the next few years except at my word" (I Ki. 17:1). Then Elijah vanished, crossing the Jordan River to live as a recluse in the Kerith Ravine, and later seeking refuge in Sidon.

For 42 months Israel saw no moisture (see Lk. 4:25; Jas. 5:17). The land was scorched, and the animals were dying from thirst. So desperate was the need that Ahab himself went out searching for water (I Ki. 18:1-6). As was natural for a man who had turned away from God, he was enraged—not at himself or his evil ways, but at the prophet Elijah who had foretold the disaster.

Finally Elijah confronted him again. Ahab's question indicates his bottled-up rage: "Are you the one who is making all this trouble?" In the face of royal anger, Elijah presented a fearless diagnosis of the case. The trouble, he said, comes from the king and his family. Elijah then seized the initiative. He commanded the king (think of that!) to assemble all the personnel of the sanctuaries of Baal and Asherah, together with a vast number of people, on the ridge of Mt. Carmel. The prophet's words were dramatic: "How long will you waver between two opinions?" The people had to choose: it must be either Yahweh or Baal!

Yahweh Answers by Fire (18:36-39)

To appreciate Elijah's prayer fully, we must look back at verses 26-28, which describe the frenzied praying of the prophets of Baal. They danced about, shouted, and finally, in desperation, gashed their flesh until their blood mingled with the blood on their cold altar.

Put yourself inside the minds of these representatives of Baal. From their background and training, these men believed that their god presided over the welfare of the Canaanite people. This must have given them a strong sense of being rooted in the life of the land. Also, those who have studied the history of Baal in Canaanite folklore tell us that Baal had once been in conflict with a rival deity, Prince Sea-Judge River, and had defeated this opponent. No doubt the prophets of Baal really believed this legend and hoped for a repetition of the triumph.

In any case, they were deeply involved in a contest. Elijah, not they, had chosen the terms and laid down the challenge. We can imagine their frustration when no fire fell on their sacrifice.

The contrast between this mindless, violent, and futile scene, and the quiet, dignified prayer of Yahweh's prophet is eloquent. The false prophets' prayers were blind repetitions, without any real content. Elijah's prayer was an appeal to the God of the universe and to His ancient promises. Elijah said "hear me" but twice—and this in deepest confidence.

Yahweh's reply to Elijah's prayer was prompt and impressive. The fire which fell was no ordinary blaze. It was, of course, a very controlled flame, for it was able to consume wood, meat, dust, and stone without harming the people. It even lapped up the water Elijah had poured on the altar.

The test was now complete. On all hands, the people cried out that Yahweh was God. Elijah then carried out an ancient command: that false prophets were to be put to death (Deut. 18:20). It was admittedly a rugged and shocking scene. But who can avoid the feeling that the situation called for strong action, as the spiritual course of God's people was at stake?

The outcome of the contest on Mt. Carmel expressed very clearly Yahweh's right to exclusive worship. This fact was quickly seen by the people, whose response was unconditional.

It is impossible for any generation to make a final commmitment for the generations that follow it. But any people can make a firm decision for their own present, and the group who witnessed the miracle on Mt. Carmel did just that.

For Discussion

1. What does it mean to you to serve the Lord with your whole heart?

2. Name three areas of your life that have the greatest potential for becoming competitors to God in your life. What practical steps can you take to insure that God receives your allegiance first in these areas?

3. Have you ever had an experience in which you sensed you were choosing between "God's way" and something else? What did you choose, and what was the result?

Window on the Word

A Wise Choice

Blaise Pascal, one of the acknowledged masters of calculus in the 16th century, was asked why he believed in eternal life. He said, "Let's assume that I am wrong and there is no life hereafter—then I have lost nothing. On the other hand, let's assume that I am right and there is life hereafter—then I have gained everything."

8

Evil in a Nation

Truth to Apply: Observing how evil enters a nation, I am challenged to become an influence for good in my own country.

Key Verse: [Omri and Ahab] did evil in the eyes of the Lord (I Kings 16:25a, 30a).

Few Americans saw so intimately the evil in modern-day national leadership as did Leon Jaworski. The well-known attorney served both as a chief prosecutor at the Nazi War Trials in Nuremberg, and as chief prosecutor in the Watergate scandal. Reflecting in his autobiography on what he saw during the Watergate trials, he observed: "But must we all not stand accountable with them as we watch the waning of morality in our country? We see the growth of white collar crime . . . the tragedy of upper and middle income people bilking insurance companies with fraudulent claims and avoiding income taxes, and news of high level government officials caught red-handed in payoff schemes.

"To combat vice, massive government investigations are launched, new legislation is introduced, and at election time the rascals are usually thrown out.

"And yet, it seems to go on and on . . .

"I see only one answer to it all: that those who profess a religious faith rededicate themselves to its principles.

"My concern now is that we are failing the Almighty" (Leon Jaworski, *Crossroads*).

Background/Overview: *I Kings 16:21-33, 22:37-39*

Omri (AHM-rye) came to power in a revolution in 885 B.C. The nation of Israel was in desperate straits after a series of brutal power struggles. They were suffering economically and militarily, especially with the rise of the Aramean kingdom in Damascus under its powerful leader Ben-hadad I. Assyria was also on the rise from Mesopotamia. Omri faced the task of developing strong alliances with Judah and Phenicia, and guarding against assault from the east. He was for the most part successful in his strategy.

Omri's new capital at Samaria was well defended. Archaeological remains have shown excellent fortifications and signs of great wealth, such as ivory inlays in buildings (see I Ki. 22:39). He also strengthened the defenses of other cities and sank tunnels into wells deep beneath fortified cities (such as the famous tunnel at Megiddo). However, the wealth that developed during Omri's and Ahab's reigns was not shared by all, and the lot of the peasantry seems to have worsened, provoking prophets like Amos. Excessive taxation from the state, usurious interest rates, and drought created great suffering among the poor.

Light on the Text

Omri's Wrong Choices (16:21-25)

"What good will it be for a man if he gains the whole world, yet forfeits his soul?" Jesus asked rhetorically (Mt. 16:26).

King Omri could have profited from such a warning. He was an able administrator and effective politician. And the times certainly required such skills. The Northern Kingdom lacked stability, was threatened by strong forces from Damascus, and was economically impoverished. Omri's success in dealing with these problems is impressive, especially since his reign lasted only 11 full years.

The archaeological evidence for Omri's importance is also impressive. For example, the Moabite stone (a black basalt stone with an inscription commemorating a Moabite rebellion against Ahab) reports on Omri's successful campaign to recover the lost territory of Moab which had successfully split off from Israel after the division of the Kingdom. Also, visitors to Megiddo may view an impressive tunnel and well system that provided water for that fortress in case of siege.

But God was not impressed with these developments. Omri's actions protected the political and economic life of Israel, but not her spiritual life. Pagan practices flourished. Micah 6:16 refers to Ahab and Omri as the epitome of corrupt religion. The influence of the local Canaanite population, substantial in the Northern Kingdom, prepared the way for the resurgence of idolatry. The missionary zeal of Jezebel eventually lead to the adoption of Baal worship as the official cult of the nation.

Ahab: Outdoing Omri (16:29-33)

While Omri's reign got six verses, the period of Ahab's reign covers almost all the remaining chapters of I Kings—not because of any virtue in Ahab. Rather, the Scriptures focus on Elijah, the adversary of Ahab and Jezebel in the battle for the hearts and minds of Israel.

The text tells us that Ahab even outdid Omri in evil, moving beyond the cultic golden calf worship of Jeroboam to the introduction of foreign deities, specifically Baal. Ahab's marriage to Jezebel became a symbol of Ahab's spiritual corruption. Jezebel's father was Ethbaal, king of Tyre and Sidon, a prominent priest of Astarte who himself had gained the throne by assassinating his brother.

It was bad enough to marry a pagan princess (in violation of the law set forth in Ex. 34:16 and Deut. 7:3), but Ahab built a temple of Baal worship for her in Samaria.

Ahab perhaps thought that he could control Jezebel and gain a political advantage without paying the price. But in him we see how one wrong step leads to another, and that unholy alliances lead to corruption. Ahab may have had the good intention of protecting Israel by the alliance with Tyre, but he was unable to resist Jezebel's desire to establish Baal worship throughout the land.

The picture we are given of Ahab is of a man not so much darkly bent on evil and corruption, as of a weak, self-indulgent person unable to resist the temptations or the pleasures of sin. Ahab had no moral fiber, no backbone to help him stand upright in a culture infiltrated with the blandishments of evil. Ahab never repudiated the Lord officially; he seems, in fact, to have had a certain furtive, fearful respect for God (I Ki. 21:27-29).

But he never stood up for God either, and he allowed himself to be influenced by foolish policy and corrupt companions.

Ahab: The Last Word (22:34-39)

Ahab's death is a fascinating story full of intrigue, deception, and judgment. It begins with Judah and Israel making an alliance to seek to recapture an important fortress city—Ramoth in Gilead—which had fallen into the hands of the Syrians. Ahab implored Jehoshaphat's assistance in the venture, but insisted they consult the prophets to see what God's word was. Ahab assembled some 400 prophets of God, yet it is clear they were "house prophets," fully prepared to say whatever Ahab wanted to hear. But Jehoshaphat rightly suspected these paid counselors and wanted a "prophet of the Lord." Ahab admitted there was such a prophet, named Micaiah (my-KAY-uh). Ahab hated Micaiah because Micaiah didn't say nice things about him. But he reluctantly agreed to call the prophet for questioning. Micaiah at first mockingly said what the king wanted to hear, but when Ahab pressed him to speak the truth, he then declared that the war would not go well. He described a vision of Heaven in which supernatural beings devised a plan to deceive the prophets into encouraging Ahab to go to battle so that he might be destroyed. To say the least, Ahab was not pleased. He had Micaiah thrown into prison until he returned from battle. But Ahab must have secretly worried, for he disguised himself (vs. 30). The ruse seemed to work, for

Jehoshaphat, appearing at the battle in Ahab's robes, was the target of the Syrian captains who had been ordered to kill only Ahab. But, alas, a soldier "drew his bow at random" and shot the fatal arrow that struck Ahab. The text then simply reports, "So the king died." He was brought back to the capital where the now bloody chariot was washed, and the dogs licked up the blood.

There was no escape. So deep had Ahab's own moral corruption sunk that he could neither stand to hear the words of a true prophet nor follow them when they came. His military power could not save him. His false prophets were useless. His attempt to disguise his identity was futile. Micaiah, at least symbolically in his vision, saw the truth—that Ahab's destruction was God's judgment. No tricks, no might were of any use. It was time for Ahab to reap what he had sown.

Making Choices

People often ask, what's the "bottom line"? The term comes from finance and accounting, and refers to the last figure in a financial report that really tells the story of success or failure. It's that "bottom line" that you really watch.

In the accounts of Omri and Ahab, the Biblical writer clearly wants us not to miss the "last word" or the bottom line. It is the final word that really passes judgment on the whole enterprise. And God's word about Ahab, His final word and bottom line, is "the king died . . . and the dogs . . ." All the glory, the alliances, the victories, the human honors carved in memorials are preliminary judgments and guesses. But the last word is that it was empty and vain.

In our own lives, and in the life of a nation, the text invites us to be wary of interim accounting. We are invited instead to recognize who has the last word—who will write the epitaph.

For Discussion

1. What issues in our nation today demand that our leaders take a strong stand—to choose moral principle

over political expediency? How can we influence them to take that stand?

2. What are some signs that might be better than the gross national product for assessing a nation's spiritual level?

3. Identify one choice you have made in the past three years that seemed small at the time, but that started you in an important new direction for your life.

Window on the Word

We'll Do It Our Way

I sat worshiping with other visitors in St. Mary's Basilica, a monolith of Roman Catholic architecture in Minneapolis. When the lay tour guide arrived, we learned that when the building had been raised in 1904 it had cost $2 million. "Maybe it will stand here for 500 years," our host mused.

One young girl had the audacity to ask, "Why do those big, square pillars in the front have 'A' and 'U' carved in them?" I looked. She'd noticed what, incredibly, I hadn't: Artisans had carved, and workmen had set into place, two mammoth granite blocks which topped off giant columns holding up the vaulted ceiling. Into the ornate scrollwork on the west side had been cut the letter "A"— the Alpha. On the other side, where Omega should have been represented, the scrollwork highlighted a rounded letter "U." It had not been simply that the block was upside down. The scrollwork could be set only one way to match the pattern on the other side. Clearly what had happened was that someone, given templates for the Alpha and Omega (but not knowing the Greek alphabet), had simply said, "This can't be right. They wouldn't want this 'U' to be carved upside down. I know how it ought to be. I'll do it my way." And he did.

And now, 75 years after the building's erection, this ornate witness to the craftman's folly stares down at 2,000 worshipers . . . and may still do so 500 years from now. We'll do it our way. To our peril. (Michael L. Sherer, *The Christian Century*)

9

Lean on Me—But Not Too Much!

Truth to Apply: I must learn the difference between having role models, and depending too heavily on someone else for faith and strength.

Key Verse: Why do you disobey the Lord's commands? You will not prosper. Because you have forsaken the Lord, he has forsaken you (II Chr. 24:20).

The poem "Casey at the Bat," by Ernest Lawrence Thayer, tells of a baseball game in which everything comes down to a slugger named Casey. The hometown fans think Casey can do no wrong. The tension mounts as Casey strikes once, then twice. Will he do it? The pitcher throws and Casey swings again . . . and misses! The game is lost, and the hometown fans are shocked: "There is no joy in Mudville." The people's faith is shattered because they leaned wholly on Casey, and Casey let them down.

Casey, in a way, symbolizes the tendency we all have at one time or another to lean too heavily on others for faith. We may talk a good game, but do we know how to play?

Joash was a good and decent king, but he leaned too heavily on his spiritual mentor, Jehoiada. When Jehoiada died, Joash stumbled as a leader.

Faith is something that can be borrowed for a while, but sooner or later the one who borrows must make an accounting. Rarely do we make a conscious effort to see who we are "borrowing" faith from, but it becomes apparent in the hour of crisis, when we are left alone, and suddenly life looms large.

When was the last time you found yourself leaning too much? What happened?

There are two key figures in this passage: Joash, king of Judah from 835 to 796 B.C., and Jehoiada, the high priest.

Jehoiada was the high priest during the reign of the evil Queen Athaliah, who preceded Joash. (Athaliah had usurped the throne after the death of her son Ahaziah. She had murdered all the royal children except the infant prince Joash, whom Jehoiada's wife rescued and concealed in the Temple for six years [II Chr. 22:10-12].)

When Joash was seven years old, Jehoiada proclaimed him king and slew Athaliah (II Chr. 23:1-15). He then led the people to make a covenant with God and with the king, and encouraged them to destroy the Baal temple (II Ki. 11:17, 18).

Under the guidance of Jehoiada, Joash instituted religious and political reforms. Baal worship was crushed, and the worship of the Lord through sacrifices was reinstated.

Joash reigned for 40 years. Jehoiada acted as advisory regent of the kingdom and as tutor to the boy king (II Ki. 12:2). II Chronicles adds the information that "Jehoiada chose two wives for him, and he had sons and daughters" (II Chr. 24:3).

Joash proved to be a good king; repairs were made on the Temple, and the system of Temple revenue was improved (II Ki. 12:5-17). The neglected Temple was, no doubt, in need of extensive repairs.

Light on the Text

Joash's Righteousness (24:1-7)

Joash was seven years old when he came to the throne. Queen Athaliah, an evil woman, had wanted to kill Joash as she had the other royal children, but Jehoiada's wife hid him in the Temple from infancy until he was six. (See II Chr. 22:10 and 24:1.) After the murder of King

Ahaziah of Judah by Jehu in his bloody revolution in the north, the throne of Judah was seized by the queen mother, Athaliah. Her six-year reign was a time of uncertainty for the people of Judah, and they were glad when Joash ascended to the throne. Not only was the Davidic dynasty imperiled by Athaliah's reign, but the worship of the Lord was endangered, for Athaliah was a devotee of Baal. Under her royal patronage Baalism flourished in the land. It is probable that this Baal was the Tyrian Baal-Melcarth. The worship of this god gained a stronghold both in the north and the south.

Jehoiada led the revolt against Queen Athaliah. When the time was ripe, he organized mercenaries, the Temple guards, and the people. The day he chose was the Sabbath, which was a holiday.

Jehoiada so arranged the guards that all three companies were present at the same time in the Temple. Then he brought in young King Joash, crowned him, and anointed him while those present shouted, "Long live the king" (II Ki. 11:12).

Hearing the shouting, Athaliah came to the Temple. She realized at once what had happened. Then, on Jehoiada's orders, she was taken outside the Temple to one of the palace gates. There she was slain (II Ki. 11:13-16).

Young King Joash immediately set out to gather monies from all Israel. Because the Temple was the property of the whole nation and the services performed in it were for the benefit of the people at large, it was only right that everyone should respond. The Temple was in a terribly dilapidated state, requiring annual contributions to fund repairs. This is the first record of such a general collection for building or repairing a house of God.

The collection referred to in II Chronicles 24:6 was the poll tax, fixed by Moses. Half a shekel was levied on every man over 20 years old. This was considered a "ransom" for their souls (e.g., a covering for their sin), that there might be no plague among them (see Ex. 30:12-14).

Jehoiada the chief priest no doubt had a great deal to do with the many key reforms done during the reign of Joash. He had won the confidence of the people and was highly regarded as a religious leader. His work to get the young king crowned and his skill in his efforts for God brought him considerable recognition from the people. In fact, he was buried among the kings of Judah in the city of David (II Chr. 24:15, 16).

Joash felt a strong sense of obligation to Jehoiada because the priest's wife, helped by her husband, had arranged sanctuary for the infant king while his life was in danger. And Jehoiada counseled Joash in his youth during the early days of his reign.

Joash's Idolatry (24:17-20)

After Jehoiada died, a significant core group of the princes of Judah "paid homage" to King Joash. Joash listened to them and under their influence allowed Judah to revert to the worship of idols. The good influence of Jehoiada appeared to be forgotten.

When Jehoiada's son, Zechariah, reprimanded him, the king commanded that the young man be stoned. The hardening effect of sin was already at work in Joash's life. He appeared to forget utterly all he owed to Zechariah's father. As Zechariah lay dying, he cried out, "May the Lord . . . call you to account." Later that same year, a small raiding party of Syrians invaded Judah and inflicted heavy damage. In the fighting, Joash was severely wounded. Later several of his servants took revenge on him for murdering Zechariah; they killed him as he slept. His son, Amaziah, ascended the throne in his stead.

There are at least three reasons for Joash's spiritual downfall. (1) He had retained the high places (the groves for idol worship). His reformation was not complete, so the germs of future evil remained. (2) He gave heed to evil counselors. (3) He disregarded the warnings of God. Joash's downfall underscores the necessity for constant watchfulness against sin. Many, like him, begin well, but end badly.

Overly Dependent upon Others

It isn't always easy to determine when we're leaning too heavily on someone else. After all, doesn't the Bible say we are to draw strength from one another, encourage one another, and help one another? Yes. Part of the beauty of the Church is the interdependency we enjoy as fellow believers in Christ. "Blest be the tie that binds" is no empty slogan; it's reality. On the other hand, there come times when we need to stand for ourselves, face the world head-on, and be mature. That was Joash's problem. He had been babied too much. He had lived so fully in the shadow of Jehoiada that, when Jehoiada faded, Joash couldn't take the heat.

List at least five persons who have had a strong influence upon you (a parent, minister, etc.).

1. _____
2. _____
3. _____
4. _____
5. _____

Now list several people over whom you have some influence.

1. _____
2. _____
3. _____
4. _____
5. _____

How would you evaluate each relationship? Were you overly dependent or was there mutual support? How do those over whom you have influence regard you? Can they stand on their own?

For Discussion

1. Have you had experiences in which God was less an influence in your decision than was some human being? What resulted?

2. How can you set an example of depending on God for your family? friends?

3. Why do you think we often tend to depend on other people rather than God for spiritual nourishment and guidance?

WINDOW ON THE WORD

A Christian First

When Millet, whose *Angelus* captivated the whole art-loving world, was about to depart from his home in Paris where he became the pupil of Delaroche, his pious grandmother said to him, "I would rather see you dead than unfaithful to God's commands." And when he was just coming into his glory as one of the greatest painters of his day, this same godly woman, whose influence made itself felt in every picture he put on the canvas, said to him, "Remember, my son, you were a Christian before you became a painter" (W. E. Biederwolf).

10

Success: Higher And Higher?

Truth to Apply: I must learn to discern the difference between worldly success and success in God's eyes.

Key Verse: You have indeed defeated Edom and now you are arrogant (II Kings 14:10a).

Pride gets the best of us into trouble. Raymond was noted for his public speaking; so when his high school class scheduled its reunion, Raymond naturally volunteered to give one of his famous addresses. He insisted on doing it from memory even though his wife knew he should carry some notes in his pocket, just in case. The night of the banquet, Raymond wished he had listened to his wife. His mind went blank. He couldn't remember a thing to say. Stories he had told for years came out flat and dull. It was a miserable—and humbling—night for Raymond.

Pride gets us into trouble when it leads us to believe that we are bigger, stronger, smarter, wiser, better, healthier, richer, nicer, kinder, purer, or holier than we really are. Such pride leads us to the precipice of reality and says, "See that big hole down there? Well, you can leap across it if you really try. You won't get hurt; you're too big, strong, and smart." Pride encourages us to take inordinate, needless risks. Pride is dangerous when it begins to control our lives.

Can you recall a time when an overdose of pride nearly killed your reputation or perhaps shattered one of your dreams?

Background/Overview: *II Kings 14:1-3, 8-14*

Amaziah came to the throne after the death of his father, King Joash. The death of Joash is important to the understanding of Amaziah's reign, for it was in retaliation for this death that Amaziah began his reign. One of the first things he did was to slay the perpetrators of his father's murder.

Joash (or Jehoash) is a name that applies to two different persons in our Scripture passage, and for that reason it can be a bit confusing. We have just mentioned Amaziah's father, Joash. The other Joash in the passage is Amaziah's opponent and counterpart in the north, King Joash of Israel. It is this Joash that plays the primary role in our story.

The situation behind the scenes here is a state of religious ambivalence and increasing moral disarray. The era of Elisha the prophet has almost come to an end. The destruction of Israel by the Assyrians is only 70 years away, and the destruction of Jerusalem by the Babylonians only about 200 years away. Solomon's Temple is still the chief center for worship in Judah, yet the groves set apart for Baal and Ashtaroth still exist throughout the country. It is an era of rapidly deteriorating social order and moral responsibility. That the two kingdoms go to war with one another is an indication of how far they had fallen from the ideals of David and Solomon.

Light on the Text

A New King on the Block (14:1-3)

When Amaziah succeeded his father, Joash, to the throne, he had visions of becoming a great king. To be a great king Amaziah would need to speak and think for himself. He would need a clear head and a vision for the future—regardless of events in the past. He would need to revere the honorable exploits of his father without unduly or unconditionally continuing them. He would need to discern what history was calling *him* to do. And he would need to be truehearted in his choice and practice of faith, not mechanical. David was great because he knew God and loved God. Yet the writers, in summarizing Amaziah's moral character and extent of his reign, seem to characterize him as something of a moral hybrid—not quite as good as King David, his great ancestor, but apparently not quite as bad as some of the other kings of the time. Like his father Joash, Amaziah was capable of being swayed. In reaching for success, he would lose sight of God and a realistic view of himself.

Put Up Your Dukes! (14:8-10)

In II Kings 14:4-7 we learn some interesting facts about Amaziah:

1. He didn't remove the pagan shrines around the Judean countryside (vs. 4).

2. He killed the murderers of his father, yet in accordance with the Law spared the lives of their children (vss. 5, 6).

3. He killed 10,000 Edomites in battle and renamed a captured city (vs. 7).

It would seem, then, that Amaziah was on the whole a law-abiding man, who believed in sharp retaliation yet took a permissive stance toward pagan worship. He ruled in anger, at least in the beginning, and soon felt a growing sense of power as a swordsman, interpreter of the Law, and protector of Judah, his homeland. While these may be worthy qualities, Amaziah apparently misread them and felt himself incapable of defeat.

Amaziah blatantly provoked and instigated the confrontation with Israel. "Come, meet me face-to-face" is a square-jawed way of challenging—"my army against yours." Jehoash was apparently wise enough to see through Amaziah's error in judgment, and set out to tell him off in a most creative manner. He wrote him a parable.

What an insult it was to call Amaziah a thistle! A thistle is a nuisance, a plant with little redeeming value. On the contrary, a cedar (Israel) is a comely tree, known throughout Lebanon for its great worth and lordly reputation. That the thistle would send to the cedar to ask for a wife is a ridiculous notion. Amaziah probably smoldered over this. Then, to make matters worse, Jehoash concluded by saying that a wild beast trampled the thistle down.

Jehoash wrote a stinging parable. But he also wrote a stinging postscript—verse 10. "Be satisfied with the victory you've got," he says in effect, "but don't mess with us. We'll mess you up good!" How many times have we heard come-ons like this in boxing circles? The champ tells the challenger to go home and be satisfied with the little trophies he has won, "but don't mess with me, or you'll get hurt." So—King A has sent a nasty letter to King B. King B has retorted with surprising cool. What will happen now? Is war in the offing?

Knockout (14:11-14)

Unfortunately for Amaziah, the parable fell on deaf ears. He resolved to meet Jehoash face-to-face in battle.

The battle took place at Beth-shemesh, a city, interestingly enough, reserved for the priestly clan, the Levites. It would seem that Jehoash was the aggressor, for it says, "So Jehoash king of Israel attacked." He drew first blood. He would not allow Amaziah to bring his army onto Israelite soil.

This, of course, made the defeat of Amaziah all the more humiliating! He would be a nonhero in his own land. The battle is described in a single sentence (vs. 12), and it is obvious that Judah was no match for Israel. The troops of Amaziah actually seem cowardly ("every man fled to his home")—the most horrible scenario Amaziah could have imagined.

But Jehoash was not through. Fulfilling, in a way, his own prophecy ("a wild beast . . . trampled the thistle"), he rode into Jerusalem with a disconsolate Amaziah in tow and proceeded to loot and destroy what Jerusalem and her people held most dear: much of the city wall (about 580 feet of it); the Temple's sacred vessels; and even the king's own "china" and silver! Plus hostages! The great king Amaziah had suffered a most unfortunate—though predictable—fall.

"Pride goes before destruction, a haughty spirit before a fall," Proverbs 16:18 says. Amaziah certainly illustrates this. He lacked the ability to accept his own limitations, and he paid for that lack.

Success: Getting It and Keeping It

Becoming successful has been one of the mainstays of modern culture—particularly since the days of World War II, but even before that. Much of the American philosophy, for example, has been built upon the premise that a people can do anything if they put their hearts and minds to it—even if it isn't always the right thing to do.

"You can be anything" certainly has a nice ring to it, but that advice can be a bit of a problem if the "anything" is outside the realm of possibility or wisdom—or both.

Amaziah didn't know how to handle his success. He made the mistake of assuming that success in one arena automatically meant success in another.

Moguls in the motion picture industry have discovered the lure of sequels. If *Fish* makes a bundle at the box office, they reason, then *Fish II* will probably make at least half that much. In reality, *Fish II* stinks, and *Fish III* isn't worth reeling in, but—if this is the formula for success, then let's make as many *Fish* as we can! At least, that's the mentality at work. And we consumers are the bait.

Rate each occupation (by marking an "x" somewhere along each line) according to the degree to which ambition for personal success enters in. How do the people in each occupation handle success?

OCCUPATION	PERSONAL SUCCESS FIGURES:		
	Greatly	Somewhat	Not at all
Acting			
Farming			
Preaching			
Doctoring			
Selling			
Governing			
Banking			
Driving			
Playing (sports)			

For Discussion

1. How is pride a problem for Christians? What can be done about it?

2. Think of ways that success has been both your friend and your enemy. How do you think God measures success?

3. Are you currently experiencing conflict between your drive for success and your desire to follow God? What steps can you take to reorder your priorities?

Window on the Word

Higher! Higher!

Jim is climbing higher and higher in the company. Promotion after promotion is rolling in. But Jim is beginning to wonder if it is worth it all. Mary Jean, his wife, is going back to work, not because she has to but because she wants to be able to do more than just listen to Jim talk about his work.

The kids are becoming less and less enchanted with Daddy's new job. At first they thought it was terrific, but now they are seeing less and less of Daddy, and the thought of another promotion makes them shudder.

Jim is caught between personal ambition and his family's wishes. He doesn't know what to do. A new opportunity for promotion is coming up in about six months, and he stands a good chance of landing it. Should he go for it?

11

In the World, But Not of It

Truth to Apply: With Christ's help, I can avoid the subtle traps of idolatry.

Key Verse: They worshiped idols, though the Lord had said, "You shall not do this" (II Ki. 17:12).

The revival that John Wesley led in the Church of England in the 1700's, which became known as Methodism, attracted many people from the working class. Wesley preached to coal miners, factory workers, and farmers, many of whom had given up on the church. This revival resulted in many improvements in British society. But Wesley also noticed a problem among the new followers of Christ.

"I fear, whenever riches have increased," he wrote in his journal, "the essence of religion has decreased in the same proportion. Therefore, I do not see how it is possible, in the nature of things, for any revival of true religion to continue long. For religion must necessarily produce both industry and frugality, and these cannot but produce riches. But as riches increase, so will pride, anger, and love of the world in all its branches."

Wesley put his finger on a problem that has plagued the Christian church all through the centuries. How do we keep our lives focused on God and not slowly shift the focus to the blessing He gives?

Background/Overview: *II Kings 17:5-18*

God punished the kingdom of Israel for her worship of heathen gods. One of these was Asherah, a nature goddess worshiped by the Canaanites as a symbol of fertility and associated with Baal. Many legends about her had been created, and she was also worshiped in other nations. Often tree trunks were used to symbolize her presence. The word *Asherim* is the plural form for symbols of this deity.

Both the kingdoms of Israel and Judah had been polluted by this idolatry. During the reign of Abijah, king of Judah, Queen Maacah had erected an idol in a grove for the worship of Asherah (I Ki 15:13). Fortunately, when her son, Asa, became king, he removed the idol. But this idolatry returned again and again, even to the point where an idol was placed in the Temple itself (II Ki. 21:7)!

In both kingdoms there were Asherim "on every high hill and under every spreading tree" (I Ki. 14:23). Thus God's judgment eventually fell.

Light on the Text

Israel's Final Destruction (17:5-9a)

The final years of the Northern Kingdom of Israel are described at the beginning of II Kings 17. Like all the kings before him, the last king, Hoshea, did evil in the sight of the Lord. For 200 years the people of the Northern Kingdom had rebelled against God, worshiping heathen gods and indulging in all forms of wickedness in disobedience to the Law of God. Hoshea did nothing to stop this.

He had become king by murdering the previous king, Pekah (II Ki. 15:30). This kind of political intrigue and violence had become common in the kingdom where God's laws had been ignored. Pekah had lost a large section of the nation to the Assyrians around 732 B.C. Israel was forced to pay tribute (usually large sums of money) each year to the king of Assyria.

When Hoshea began his reign, he continued to pay this tribute, but then foolishly decided to rebel. He stopped the payments and tried to set up an alliance with the Egyptian king to fight against Assyria. A new Assyrian king, Shalmaneser, then decided to crush Israel once and for all. After laying siege to Samaria, the capital city, for three years, he conquered the nation and removed most of the people to some distant places in the Assyrian Empire. Possibly as many as 27,000 people were deported from Israel.

From a political and military point of view, Hoshea's rebellion against Assyria was hopeless. The Assyrians maintained a huge standing army. Nations that challenged their power were not only destroyed, but their people were scattered to other places in the empire. Both Israel and Judah were too weak to resist the Assyrians, and they had previously learned to make their peace with Assyria. Political alliances with other nations to fight against Assyria always ended in disaster.

From God's point of view, Israel's captivity was His judgment of their sin. Verses 7-23 review this failure of the Northern Kingdom, showing why God's punishment was necessary.

Their sin against God was twofold. First, they rebelled against God. They committed personal sins that were contrary to His standards in the Law (vs. 9). They forgot that God had chosen them to be His people and redeemed them from Egypt to live in holiness before Him and before the nations of the world.

Second, they followed after false gods. They were influenced by heathen customs and beliefs—exactly what God had warned them against when they settled in Canaan. The kings of Israel also introduced their own customs and ways of worship that were not in keeping with God's Law (vs. 8).

Israel's Sin of Idolatry (7:12-15a, 17, 18)

These verses continue to focus on the idolatry of the Northern Kingdom. The prophet Hosea, who spoke against the unfaithfulness of Israel toward God, declared, "Ephraim [Israel] is joined to idols" (Hos. 4:17). He cried out God's message: "I know all about

Ephraim; Israel is not hidden from me. Ephraim, you have now turned to prostitution; Israel is corrupt" (Hos. 5:3). In God's eyes, idolatry was a form of adultery. To worship foreign gods was an act of unfaithfulness to Him. To pursue the pleasures of this world without any regard to God's demands for holy living was like being a prostitute.

Hosea's own personal experience symbolized this unfaithfulness. God told him to marry a woman named Gomer (Hos. 1:2, 3). She was unfaithful to him and spurned every effort of Hosea to restore her to the loving relationship of marriage. Gomer became a picture of the Northern Kingdom. God's mercy was offered repeatedly to the nation through His prophets—Elijah, Elisha, and Amos—but the kings and the people refused to accept it. They continued in their sin and rebellion.

We have already noted the perversion of the true worship of God that Jeroboam and his successors instituted in the Northern Kingdom. The influence of numerous foreign deities was just as offensive to God.

One of the most hideous was the worship of Moloch. To appease this god, children were sacrificed. Apparently some of this was happening in Israel (II Ki. 17:17), a direct violation of God's law against such practices (Deut. 18:10). Astrology, magic, and sun worship were also practiced in Israel—all in disobedience to God.

There were remnants of Baal worship to be found, in spite of Jehu's determined effort to eradicate this cult (II Ki. 10:24-28) and Elijah's direct attack on Ahab's use of this false religion (I Ki. 18:40).

The most popular goddess, however, was Asherah, the Assyrian fertility symbol. Idols of wood in her image were found all over Israel where people could worship her (II Ki. 17:10). Fertility gods and goddesses were often associated with sexual activity; and in the name of these false religions, sexual promiscuity was encouraged. Temple prostitutes were common.

All this idolatry polluted the nation and angered God (vs. 18). Why? God could see the emptiness of Israel's idolatry, the utter uselessness of these false religions; His holiness was mocked by His people's degradation; His offer of a covenantal relationship of love and intimacy with His people was continually rejected.

Throughout the Bible, God refers to Himself as a jealous God. He is jealous for the love of His people. Anything that comes between Him and His people is, in fact, an idol (Deut. 32:21).

Idolatry Today?

Idolatry is not limited to ancient societies. We—twentieth-century Westerners are often just as idolatrous, even though we've never bowed down to a statue or sacrificed an animal.

That's because an idol is anything that takes the exclusive place intended for God Himself in our lives. Any substitute for God is an idol, and treating anything or anyone like God is idolatry.

Possible categories of idolatry are material possessions, personal pleasures, ways of exercising power over others, occult involvement, family or friends, comfort.

But can our church life become idolatrous? Indeed it can. Some people, for example, view size and variety of church programs as measures of success. A program can be a way to impress others and make the members feel important. Another idol can be habit or tradition. Over a span of time, people can forget the original objective of a program. The program is maintained for its own sake, regardless of its effectivemess. Finally, programs—even church programs—can be shields to prevent a confrontation with God. Even Bible classes can be idols by encouraging students to be more concerned with knowing *about* God than knowing God Himself.

For Discussion

1. What kinds of advertising are you susceptible to: food, automobiles, beverages, cosmetics, tourist attractions? Much contemporary advertising does more than inform us of products that are available. It also tries to create a want or desire in us for the product, even if we don't really need it. What makes advertising such a powerful influence? What steps can we take to resist, and help our children resist, the lure of advertising?

2. If material blessings are from God, how can they become idols? How can we enjoy them properly?

3. What do you think is the greatest area of idolatry in our country? Your church? Your life?

Window on the Word

Modern Idolatry

". . . when I talk about worshiping the golden cow, I am talking about a particular form of materialism to which we have fallen prey. It is a way of life that sets our feet on the road to spiritual harlotry.

"And it is precisely here, in our unconscious acceptance of a false value system (with its confusion about our "rights") that the root of the problem lies. Here lies the weakness that makes us prone to spiritual harlotry. For we have overvalued material prosperity and have underestimated, taken for granted, or even forgotten, the God of power and love we profess to worship. We claim to have faith in Him. But so long as we are harassed by anxiety about our financial security or overly impressed by the importance of money in Christian work, our profession is hollow and our footsteps follow the pathway to whoredom." (John White, *The Golden Cow*)

12

Making Dreams Come True

Truth to Apply: I am called to turn my talents and gifts over to God to be used by Him for fruit bearing in my life.

Key Verse: Once more a remnant of the house of Judah will take root below and bear fruit above (II Ki. 19:30).

*A poor Mexican boy came to faith in Jesus Christ. Then, unbelievably, God called him to preach. He lacked money, education, contacts. But he was determined to do God's will. When a church let him preach, his own mother was the first to be converted. Years later, he would travel throughout the land, telling others of Jesus. His name: Angel Martinez.

*As a teenager, he was making big money with his own jazz band. Then he accepted Christ, and eventually entered the ministry. Driving back from his first church services, he would turn his radio to the pulsating jazz, stop the car, and sob with longing. But he held true. Today he is a faithful pastor. His name: John Bisagno.

*God sent David Wilkerson into the life of a young hoodlum. He was a street fighter and gang leader, experienced in drugs and prostitution. But God's Holy Spirit eventually broke through. He devoted his new life to telling people about the Jesus who loved him even when he was in the depths of sin. His name: Nicky Cruz.
   In your own life experience, in what ways has God's power proven to be life changing?

Background/Overview: *II Kings 18—20*

Hezekiah's father, Ahaz, had avoided the ruin which came to the Northern Kingdom by becoming a vassal of the Assyrian king, Tiglath-Pileser. It is possible that a part of his submission was to introduce the worship of the Assyrian gods into the Temple in Jerusalem. As if that were not bad enough, he also allowed the native pagan practices to flourish, even on one occasion, offering a son as a sacrifice, apparently in fulfillment of some vow.

Hezekiah, Ahaz's son, was about 17 when the Northern Kingdom fell to the Assyrians, and 25 when he ascended the throne himself. Growing up in his father's court as he did, his repudiation of idolatry and his personal revival of pure worship are nothing short of amazing. To be sure, the religious situation in Judah was not as bad as it had been in Israel; prophets like Hosea and Amos painted a much bleaker picture for the Northern Kingdom. But Isaiah and Micah make it clear (see, for example, Isa. 1:10-17; Mic. 1:5, 13) that, if the situation was not as bad, it was merely a matter of degree.

Though nationalism certainly played a part in Hezekiah's reforms, it seems safe to say that the real motivating force was a desire to return to the Covenant God. That the reforms were no mere superficial whitewash is made clear by the account of Hezekiah's reign in II Chronicles 29—31.

Light on the Text

A Life Dedicated to God (18:1-8)

Although Ahaz had set up the images and idols to promote heathen worship, Hezekiah boldly tore them down. These "high places" were places to worship idols—an affront to God, and a breach of the Covenant. Hezekiah chose God's Word over following the example of his predecessors and demolished everything that defied the worship of the one, true God. Then he made a law suppressing the use of them, and executed this law with vigor. Seeing God's terrible judgment upon the kingdom of Israel may have been an important lesson for Hezekiah and his people.

Hezekiah broke the brass serpent into pieces even though it had originally been mandated by God. The children of Israel had brought it with them to Canaan as a memorial of God's goodness to their forefathers in the wilderness. But, as so often happens, they began to love the creature more than the Creator, so Hezekiah told the people that it was *Nehushtan*, "just a piece of brass." What was originally a good object, but idolized, had become evil, and the only solution was to get rid of it.

Hezekiah was unique—there was none like him, before or after. In reforming the kingdom he stood out in two ways: (1) He placed his confidence in God and, with great courage, took a stand for the right. When he became king, his kingdom was surrounded by enemies. He might have turned for help to foreign lands as his father did. Instead he trusted in God, seeking divine guidance. (2) He persevered and remained faithful— those two characteristics marked his reign. The Scriptures are full of stories of kings who made a great start, then fell away. But Hezekiah was not one of them. He stuck with it.

Receives Specific Instructions (19:29-31)

The Assyrian army had devoured all of the foodstuffs, and provisions were scarce. The vineyards were ravaged and trampled, the olive groves cut down. The remnant might well have wondered how they were going to survive. But God's instructions were specific. God instructed them to eat what grew of itself. The Assyrians had gathered what had been sown. God's people would reap what they had not sown.

A sabbatical year was coming up, and the land needed to rest, so there would be no sowing or reaping that year. But Jehovah would again provide for them with no effort on their part. After all, the land had originally been fruitful before there were people to till it (Gen. 1:11). The same God was still in control, still able to provide.

The third year they would return to the normal reaping and sowing. God also promised that the remnant would again be established, in their own country and in their own homes. They would take root downward, and bear fruit upward. God promised that the king of Assyria would not come into the city, nor shoot an arrow there. God Himself undertook to defend His people.

And Does Mighty Things (20:20)

As Hezekiah's life came to an end, he was honored greatly. Among his accomplishments is the construction of the Siloam tunnel. The American explorer Robinson mentions this tunnel in 1838, but it was not cleared until 1880, when an inscription was discovered at the point where the miners working from one end met those excavating from the other, 300 feet underneath the surface. Though only six lines remain, this is the second longest monumental text in early Hebrew (now in the Istanbul Museum). It records the work done on the 1,749-foot-long watercourse:

". . . This is the account of the mining work. While the men were swinging their axes, each toward his fellow, and while there was still three cubits (4½ feet) to be cut through, the voice of one man calling to the other was heard, showing that he was deviating to the right. When the tunnel was driven through, the excavators met man to man, axe against axe, and the water flowed for 1,200 cubits from the spring to the reservoir. The height of the rock above the heads of the excavators was 100 cubits" (D. J. Wiseman and Edwin Yamauchi, *Archaeology and the Bible*).

Hezekiah's greatness came from his willingness to put his natural talents to serving God. He was talented, but no more than other kings. What stands out in Hezekiah's case is his determination to serve God. That made him a blessing and made him great.

Youthful Dedication

The Western world has become obsessed with youth. Some products are advertised primarily on their ability to retain or restore youthfulness. The implicit thought is that with youth go prosperity, joy, and fun.

Hezekiah was young, only 25, and had plenty of time and opportunity for "enjoying" life. But he chose something different. He could have enjoyed the "pleasures of sin for a short time" (compare Heb. 11:25). But he knew where real value lay.

Hezekiah's strong point was his reforming zeal. He cleared away and destroyed the idols that were being used in defiance of the worship of the true God. When Hezekiah opened the doors of the Temple and brought true worship back, God began to bless him mightily.

But when everything was going well and God was prospering Hezekiah and the nation of Judah, trouble appeared in the form of King Sennacherib of Assyria, who determined to destroy Judah. The believer will also have trials and testings in this life. But God will still be there. Trouble may not always be a sign of God's disfavor. It may be a blessing in disguise.

For Discussion

1. Hezekiah allowed nothing to hinder him from obeying God—not youth, nor inexperience, nor opposition. Are there things hindering you from the same single-minded devotion? How can you overcome them?

2. Why was Hezekiah so confident that God would supply his people's needs? What gives you confidence in God's promises?

3. Think of one talent or gift you have. How is God refining and sharpening that gift? Do you have a dream concerning how this gift could be used? Write it down . . . perhaps as a prayer.

Window on the Word

How to Face Difficulties?

Sologdin, one of Aleksandr Solzhenitsyn's characters in his novel *The First Circle*, observed: "How to face difficulties? . . . Difficulties must be viewed as the hidden treasure! Usually the more difficult, the better. It's not as valuable if your difficulties stem from your own inner struggles. But when difficulties arise out of increasing objective resistance, that's marvelous! . . . Overcoming the increased difficulties is all the more valuable because in failure the growth of the person performing the task takes place in proportion to the difficulty encountered."

13

The Power of the Word

Truth to Apply: Acting on God's truth can renew my spiritual life.

Key Verse: I have found the Book of the Law in the temple of the Lord (II Kings 22:8b).

The man appears healthy and strong, but he feels a little strange. He has periods of weakness and dizziness. He pretends that nothing is bothering him and hopes the problems will go away. Finally, after several weeks of discomfort, he goes to a doctor. He is told that he is suffering from a rare disease which, if not treated at a hospital immediately, will probably be fatal.

This man has been faced with a choice: a life-or-death choice. He must decide whether to accept or reject the doctor's evaluation. If he refuses to accept the truth concerning his condition, he may never get well. He may ask for a second opinion and seek for alternative cures, but eventually he must face up to his condition.

Have you ever been faced with a critical decision? How did you handle it?

The Temple was, for the Jewish people, the symbol of the very presence of God. Thus, when King Josiah worked on restoring the Temple, he was seeking to restore the nation's faith.

Josiah and his people, "from the least to the greatest" (II Ki. 23:2), were able to rebuild their nation because they faced and accepted the truth about their condition. Once the truth was accepted, the building could begin.

For the young king and his people, rebuilding the Temple and the country took great effort. The Temple rebuilding demanded money, hard work, and know-how. Skilled craftsmen, carpenters, and stonemasons were employed to refurbish God's house (II Ki. 22:6).

The spiritual rebuilding of the kingdom of Judah was a different sort of building project. It demanded spiritual resolve rather than physical strength; godly values in place of artistic skills. Under Josiah's guidance, Judah destroyed the groves and altars which were dedicated to other gods. Some of those altars had been around since Solomon's reign, and Josiah worked hard to destroy them and break the long tradition of worshiping foreign gods.

Light on the Text

Finding the Word (22:10-13)

The young king Josiah did not "make waves" politically for several years. During the early years of his reign Judah was well entrenched as a vassal of Assyria. For the better part of the seventh century, Assyria's powerful king, Ashurbanipal, ruled over Judah. Manasseh, an earlier king of Judah and Josiah's grandfather (II Ki. 21), was especially used by Assyria. He allowed foreign religion and politics to literally take over Judah and its capital city, Jerusalem.

When Josiah was 18 years old, Ashurbanipal was near death. With his death, Assyria lost much of its power over Judah and the other captive nations. With the lessening of Assyria's political power, the young king of Judah had the freedom to work on the Temple. This was a wise attempt by Josiah and his advisers: to strengthen Judah by putting the Temple—and the nation's faith—in order.

During the Temple repairs, Hilkiah the high priest came to Shaphan the scribe with earthshaking news: "I have found the Book of the Law in the temple of the Lord" (vs. 8). Shaphan, in turn, delivered the news of the Book to the young king. This chain of events started the most radical spiritual reform ever to come to Judah.

As Shaphan the scribe read this newly discovered Book of the Law before the king, the boy king "tore his robes" (vs. 11). In doing this, Josiah was indicating that he and his people were guilty of personal and national disobedience. The king's rending of his clothes was a symbol of remorse and consternation. He then demanded verification of this claim. Instead of trying to study the Book's age and authorship, as modern scholars would do, the priests turned to Huldah the prophetess (vs. 14). She was evidently known and trusted as a true prophetess of God.

Josiah took the newly discovered Book seriously. His attitude toward the Book was not flippant or casual. God's Word will always stand up to our puny attempts to examine or verify. Josiah wanted to believe the Book, but he didn't want to accept any claim blindly.

Measured by the Word (22:15, 16)

Scholars have often wondered why the group delegated by Josiah went to the prophetess Huldah. In doing so they bypassed important and famous men like Zephaniah, Jeremiah, and Habakkuk. Males usually filled the office of prophet in those days, but in this case Huldah was God's mouthpiece.

The prophetess Huldah had been asked to respond to the Book which had been found. Like the old joke about having "good news" and "bad news," Huldah had some of both in her words to the king and the priests. Her message started with "This is what the Lord . . . says" (vs. 15) and contained the promise that God would indeed bring "disaster on this place and its people" (vs. 16).

Huldah verified the Book by simply adding her warning of judgment to the Book's warnings: "Because they have forsaken me and burned incense to other gods and provoked me to anger by all the idols their hands have made, my anger will burn against this place and will not be quenched" (vs. 17). Huldah measured the kingdom against God's revelation to her. Clearly she found that the people of Judah had not lived up to God's laws.

However, not all of Huldah's news was bad, as we see from God's message to Josiah. The message was that God had heard him weep and had seen him rend his clothes. God was impressed by Josiah's tender heart and his true humility (vs. 19) and gave him this personal promise: "Therefore, I will gather you to your fathers, and you will be buried in peace. Your eyes will not see all the disaster I am going to bring on this place" (vs. 20).

The Scripture clearly shows the positive response of God toward Josiah. Huldah's words verified the truthfulness of the Book, the evil in Judah's past, and the godliness of Josiah. God's judgment would indeed fall harshly upon Judah. Josiah's sincere desire to reform could not stop God's wrath, but a generation of reformers could postpone the judgment.

It is obvious that God was very angry toward the people of Judah. His wrath was overwhelming, and threatened to spill over into violent punishment. Yet in this case God was willing to set aside His judgment for a time because of the faithfulness of one man. As a nation, Judah deserved to receive the wrath of God; but as an individual, Josiah did not deserve such treatment.

Performing the Word (23:1-3)

All along the way, King Josiah had taken the words of the newly discovered Book of the Law very seriously. With Huldah's words ringing in his ears, Josiah called a covenant meeting with all of the people. In calling the people together to read the Book of the Law, Josiah was already beginning to obey it. He gathered the people around him and read to them from the scroll which Hilkiah had found in the Temple.

This covenant service was Josiah's answer to God's command that the Book be read. He was taking the lead in making a covenant to live obediently before God.

Josiah "stood by the pillar" (vs. 3) during the service. Evidently worship custom required that the king stand by a pillar (or, some versions read, "on the platform") when representing the people of God. Josiah was following in the footsteps of King Jehoiada: "there was the king, standing by the pillar, as the custom was . . . Jehoiada then made a covenant between the Lord and the king and people" (II Ki. 11:14, 17).

The covenant which Josiah made betweeen the Lord and the king and the people included promises to follow the Lord and to keep God's commandments, testimonies, and statutes. The people were to do these things "with all [their] heart and all [their] soul" (vs. 3).

A covenant between God and His people was not something to be taken lightly. A covenant was a serious agreement. The people were agreeing to follow God—to rebuild the Temple and their country in God's image. Young King Josiah brought the people together in order to make the covenant, and then worked with them to clean up Judah.

No Other Word

Pagan worship had been purged from Israel and Judah many times before, always to return. Judah was filled with centers of pagan worship, and young King Josiah, in his twelfth year of ruling, attempted to remove them from the land. He specifically destroyed the following religions (23:4-20):

Baal and Asherah worship (23:4-10, 13, 14)
Josiah burned all of the vessels and idols that were used in the worship of Baal. He had the shrines and high places torn down.

Molech worship (23:10)
Ahaz evidently brought the worship of Molech into Judah. These religious rites were associated with human sacrifice. Josiah "desecrated" their place of worship with fire.

Astral worship (23:11, 12)
Josiah destroyed the places and objects which were being used to worship the various heavenly bodies.

High places (23:13, 14)
These special places had been built by King Solomon for the worship of strange gods by his wives. Josiah destroyed and desecrated these sites. Desecration usually included the scattering of ashes and bones on sacred ground, making them unfit for use by the superstitious worshipers.

The altar at Bethel
Josiah's religious purge was carried into the region of the former Northern Kingdom. Again, this altar was being used for a "high place" to worship pagan gods.

Josiah's attempts at reform were not all destructive. One of the king's most important moves was to command the people to celebrate a Passover feast (23:21-23). The Passover was Judah's most important annual feast. It reminded the people of the constant mercy of God. "Not since the days of the judges who led Israel, nor throughout the days of the kings of Israel and the kings of Judah, had any such Passover been observed" (23:22).

King Josiah reigned in Judah for 31 years (22:1) and worked very diligently to recover Judah for God. The writer of II Kings gives high marks to Josiah: "Neither before nor after Josiah was there a king like him who turned to the Lord as he did—with all his heart and with all his soul and with all his strength, in accordance with all the Law of Moses" (23:25).

For Discussion

1. The discovery of the Book of the Law radically changed the lives of Josiah and his people. How has the Word of God changed your life personally? Recall a moment when the Scripture penetrated your heart.

2. Josiah and the people of Judah made a covenant before the Lord. What kind of covenants can we make today—as individuals, as families, as church bodies?

3. What specifically in your spiritual life needs to be rebuilt today?

Window on the Word

The Life of Beginning Again

Christianity begins where everything else ends—it begins with death. Life in Christ involves a death, a birth, and a new beginning: "Dead indeed unto sin, but alive unto God." Paul could write in Galatians 2:20, "I am crucified with Christ: nevertheless I live; yet not I, but Christ liveth in me." The new birth is the very heart and core of Christianity. From the Fall to Calvary every movement of God was designed to carry out and consummate the provisions for the new birth.

The new birth is the reason for Judaism with its feasts, sacrifices, and chanting priests. "The law was a schoolmaster to bring us to Christ."

The new birth is the reason for the prophets with flaming words and daring courage.

The new birth is the reason for Bethlehem's manger, for Gethsemane's bloody sweat, and Calvary's terrible agony.

The hope of the world is the new birth—resurrection with Christ—nothing less will do, and nothing more is necessary. (Oliver Wilson, *Boundless Horizons*)

Leader Helps and Lesson Plan

General Guidelines for Group Study

*Open and close each session with prayer.

*Since the lesson texts are not printed in the book, group members should have their Bibles with them for each study session.

*As the leader, prepare yourself for each session through personal study (during the week) of the Bible text and lesson. On notepaper, jot down any points of interest or concern as you study. Jot down your thoughts about how God is speaking to you through the text, and how He might want to speak to the entire group. Look up cross-reference passages (as they are referred to in the lessons), and try to find answers to questions that come to your mind. Also, recall stories from your own life experience that could be shared with the group to illustrate points in the lesson.

*Try to get participation from everyone. Get to know the more quiet members through informal conversation before and after the sessions. Then, during the study, watch for nonverbal signs (a change in expression or posture) that they would like to respond. Call on them. Say: "What are your thoughts on this, Sue?"

*Don't be afraid of silence. Adults need their own space. Often a long period of silence after a question means the group has been challenged to do some real thinking—hard work that can't be rushed!

*Acknowledge each contribution. No question is a dumb question. Every comment, no matter how "wrong," comes from a worthy person, who needs to be affirmed as valuable to the group. Find ways of tactfully accepting the speaker while guiding the discussion back on track: "Thank you for that comment, John; now what do some of the others think?" or, "I see your point, but are you aware of . . . ?"

When redirecting the discussion, however, be sensitive to the fact that sometimes the topic of the moment *should be* the "sidetrack" because it hits a felt need of the participants.

*Encourage *well-rounded* Christian growth. Christians are called to grow in knowledge of the Word, but they are also challenged to grow in love and wisdom. This means that they must constantly develop in their ability to wisely apply the Bible knowledge to their experience.

Lesson Plan

The following four-step lesson plan can be used effectively for each chapter, varying the different suggested approaches from lesson to lesson.

STEP 1: *Focus on Life Need*

The opening section of each lesson is an anecdote, quote, or other device designed to stimulate sharing on how the topic relates to practical daily living. There are many ways to do this. For example, you might list on the chalkboard the group's answers to: "How have you found this theme relevant to your daily life?" "What are your past successes, or failures, in this area?" "What is your present level of struggle or victory with this?" "Share a story from your own experience relating to this topic."

Sharing questions are designed to be open-ended and allow people to talk about themselves. The questions allow for sharing about past experiences, feelings, hopes and dreams, fears and anxieties, faith, daily life, likes and dislikes, sorrows and joys. Self-disclosure results in group members' coming to know each other at a more intimate level. This kind of personal sharing is necessary to experience deep affirmation and love.

However you do it, the point is to get group members to share *where they are now* in relation to the Biblical topic. As you seek to get the group involved, remember the following characteristics of good sharing questions:[1]

1. Good sharing questions encourage risk without forcing participants to go beyond their willingness to respond.

2. Good sharing questions begin with low risk and build toward higher risk. (It is often good, for instance, to ask a history question to start, then build to present situations in people's lives.)

3. Sharing questions should not require people to confess their sins or to share only negative things about themselves.

4. Questions should be able to be answered by every member of the group.

5. The questions should help the group members to know one another better and learn to love and understand each other more.

6. The questions should allow for enough diversity in response so each member does not wind up saying the same thing.

7. They should ask for sharing of self, not for sharing of opinions.

STEP 2: *Focus on Bible Learning*

Use the "Light on the Text" section for this part of the lesson plan. Again, there are a number of ways to get group members involved, but the emphasis here is more on learning Bible content than on applying it. Below are some suggestions on how to proceed. The methods could be varied from week to week.

*Lecture on important points in the Bible passage (from your personal study notes).

*Assign specific verses in the Bible passage to individuals. Allow five or ten minutes for them to jot down 1) questions, 2) comments, 3) points of concern raised by the text. Then have them share in turn what they have written down.

*Pick important or controversial verses from the passage. In advance, do a personal study to find differences of interpretation among commentators. List and explain these "options" on a blackboard and invite comments concerning the relative merits of each view. Summarize and explain your own view, and challenge other group members to further study.

*Have class members do their own outline of the Bible passage. This is done by giving an original title to each section, chapter, and paragraph, placing each under its appropriate heading according to subject matter. Share the outlines and discuss.

*Make up your own sermons from the Bible passage. Each sermon could include: Title, Theme Sentence, Outline, Illustration, Application, Benediction. Share and discuss.

*View works of art based on the text. Discuss.

*Individually, or as a group, paraphrase the Bible passage in your own words. Share and discuss.

*Have a period of silent meditation upon the Bible passage. Later, share insights.

STEP 3: *Focus on Bible Application*

Most adults prefer group discussion above any other learning method. Use the "For Discussion" section for each lesson to guide a good discussion on the lesson topic and how it relates to felt needs.

Students can benefit from discussion in a number of important ways:[2]

1. Discussion stimulates interest and thinking, and helps students develop the skills of observation, analysis, and hope.

2. Discussion helps students clarify and review what they have learned.

3. Discussion allows students to hear opinions that are more mature and perhaps more Christlike than their own.

4. Discussion stimulates creativity and aids students in applying what they have learned.

5. When students verbalize what they believe and are forced to explain or defend what they say, their convictions are strengthened and their ability to share what they believe with others is increased.

There are many different ways to structure a discussion. All have group interaction as their goal. All provide an opportunity to share in the learning process.

But using different structures can add surprise to a discussion. It can mix people in unique ways. It can allow new people to talk.

Total Class Discussion

In some small classes, all students are able to participate in one effective discussion. This can build a sense of class unity, and it allows everyone to hear the wisdom of peers. But in most groups, total class discussion by itself is unsatisfactory because there is usually time for only a few to contribute.

Buzz Groups

Small groups of three to ten people are assigned any topic for discussion. They quickly select a chairperson and a secretary. The chairperson is responsible for keeping the discussion on track, and the secretary records the group's ideas, reporting the relevant ones to the total class.

Brainstorming

Students, usually in small groups, are presented with a problem and asked to come up with as many different solutions as possible. Participants should withhold judgment until all suggestions (no matter how creative!) have been offered. After a short break, the group should pick the best contribution from those suggested and refine it. Each brainstorming group will present its solution in a total class discussion.

Forum Discussion

Forum discussion is especially valuable when the subject is difficult and the students would not be able to participate in a meaningful discussion without quite a bit of background. People with special training or experience have insights which would not ordinarily be available to the students. Each forum member should prepare a three- to five-minute speech and be given uninterrupted time in which to present it. Then students should be encouraged to interact with the speakers, either directly or through a forum moderator.

Debate

As students prepare before class for their parts in a debate, they should remember that it is the affirmative side's repsonsibility to prove that the resolve is correct. The negative has to prove that it isn't. Of course, the negative may also want to present an alternative proposal.

There are many ways to structure a debate, but the following pattern is quite effective.
1. First affirmative speech
2. First negative speech
3. Second affirmative speech
4. Second negative speech
(brief break while each side plans its rebuttal)
5. First negative rebuttal
6. First affirmative rebuttal
7. Second negative rebuttal
8. Second affirmative rebuttal.

Floating Panel

Sometimes you have a topic to which almost everyone in the room would have something to contribute, for example: marriage, love, work, getting along with people. For a change of pace, have a floating panel: four or five people, whose names are chosen at random, will become "experts" for several minutes. These people sit in chairs in the front of the room while you and other class members ask them questions. The questions should be experience related. When the panel has been in front for several minutes, enough time for each person to make several comments, draw other names and replace the original members.

Interview As Homework

Ask students to interview someone during the week and present what they learned in the form of short reports the following Sunday.

Interview in Class

Occasionally it is profitable to schedule an in-class interview, perhaps with a visiting missionary or with someone who has unique insights to share with the group. One person can take charge of the entire interview, structuring and asking questions. But whenever possible the entire class should take part. Each student should write a question to ask the guest.

In-Group Interview

Divide the class into groups of three, called triads. Supply all groups with the same question or discussion topic. A in the group interviews B while C listens. Then B interviews C while A listens. Finally C interviews A while B listens. Each interview should take from one to three minutes. When the triads return to the class, each person reports on what was heard rather than said.

Following every class period in which you use discussion, ask yourself these questions to help determine the success of your discussion time:

1. In what ways did this discussion contribute to the group's understanding of today's lesson?

2. If each person was not involved, what can I do next week to correct the situation?

3. In what ways did content play a role in the discussion? (I.e., people were not simply sharing off-the-top-of-their-head opinions.)

4. What follow-up, if any, should be made on the discussion? (For example, if participants showed a lack of knowledge, or misunderstanding in some area of Scripture, you may want to cover this subject soon during the class hour. Or, if they discussed decisions they were making or projects they felt the class should be involved in, follow-up outside the class hour may be necessary.)

STEP 4: *Focus on Life Response*

This step tries to incorporate a bridge from the Bible lesson to actual daily living. It should be a *specific* suggestion as to "how we are going to *do* something about this," either individually, or as a group. Though this is a goal to aim for, it is unlikely that everyone will respond to every lesson. But it is good to have a suggested life response ready for that one or two in the group who may have been moved by *this* lesson to respond *this week* in a tangible way.

Sometimes a whole group will be moved by one particular lesson to do a major project in light of their deepened understanding of, and commitment to, God's will. Such a response would be well worth the weeks of study that may have preceded it.

Examples of life response activities:

1. A whole class, after studying Scriptural principles of evangelism, decides to host an outreach Bible study in a new neighborhood.

2. As a result of studying one of Paul's prayers for the Ephesians, a group member volunteers to start and oversee a church prayer chain for responding to those in need.

3. A group member invites others to join her in memorizing the key verse for the week.

4. Two group members, after studying portions of the Sermon on the Mount, write and perform a song about peacemaking.

Obviously, only you and your group can decide how to respond appropriately to the challenge of living for Christ daily. But the possibilities are endless.

[1]From *Using the Bible in Groups,* by Roberta Hestenes.
© Roberta Hestenes 1983. Adapted and used by permission of Westminster Press, Philadelphia, PA.
[2]The material on discussion methods is adapted from *Creative Teaching Methods,* by Marlene D. LeFever, available from your local Christian bookstore or from David C. Cook Publishing Co., 850 N. Grove Ave., Elgin, IL 60120. Order number: 25254. $14.95. This book contains step-by-step directions for dozens of methods appropriate for use in adult classes.